THE PYRENEES

THE PYRENEES

BOB GIBBONS

PAUL DAVIES

B.T. Batsford Ltd

ISBN 0 7134 5942 5

Typeset by Servis Filmsetting Ltd, Manchester

Printed in Great Britain by
Butler & Tanner, Frome, Somerset
for the publishers
B.T. Batsford Ltd
4 Fitzhardinge Street
London W1H 0AH

All black and white photographs are by Bob
Gibbons.

Frontispiece
The Aigues-Tortes National Park is easily reached
by car or bike; private cars are not allowed far into
the park

Contents

List of Black and White Illustrations

List of Colour Plates

(between pages 64 and 65)

Atlantic Ocean

FRANCE

● Biarritz

● Pau

● Tarbes

● Pamplona

Pic du Midi d'Ossau
△

Pic de Vignemale
△

● Gavarnie

Bagnères
de Luchon
●

△
Mt. Perdido

Jaca ●

Pico de A

THE PYRENEES

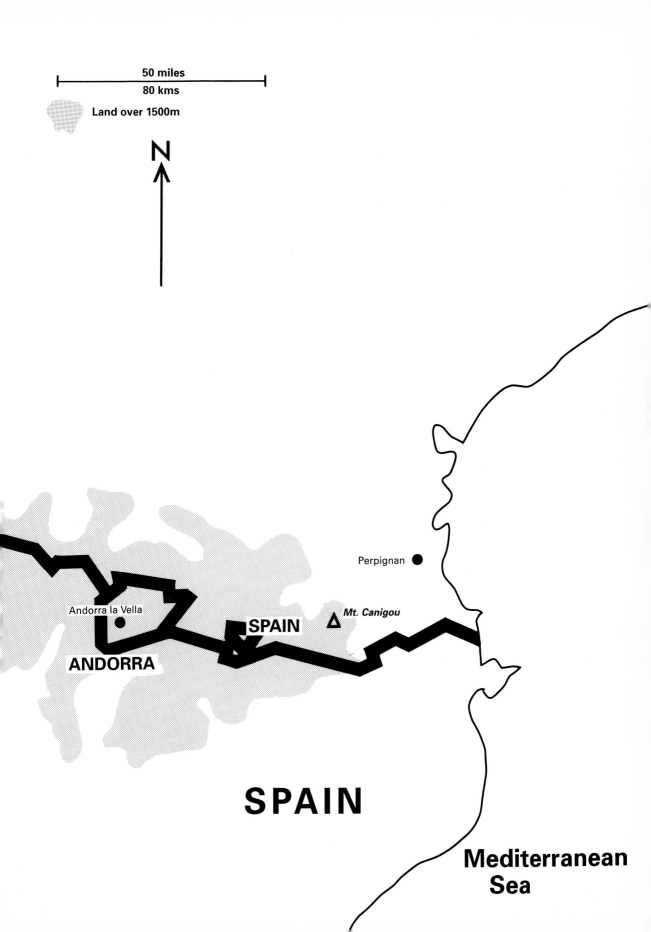

CHAPTER ONE

Introduction

For some reason, the Pyrenees are often dismissed as a poor relation to the Alps, or simply as a boundary to be negotiated on the way to or from Spain. Yet, to our minds, they are one of the most exciting areas of Europe, with exceptional landscapes, high peaks, beautiful valleys, some of the wildest and most extensive forest in Europe, excellent weather (by mountain standards!), good food, friendly, interesting people, and exceptional wildlife. Nowadays, with such good roads, they are very accessible, and we have often left a Channel port in the morning and reached the Pyrenees in time to find accommodation in the evening.

Although the Pyrenees are often perceived simply as a 'wall' dividing Spain from France, this gives a misleading impression of the depth of their interest. The French slopes rise rapidly to the high peaks, but the Spanish side is far more complex, falling away gradually to the south in a series of ranges. In addition, the Pyrenees are by no means the straight line they are often depicted as, and the central area is a complex of high peaks, outlying massifs and overlapping ranges. This makes them far more rewarding and exciting to visit, for there are hidden valleys and peaks; long steadily-climbing valleys through beech, fir and pine forests; high pastures, isolated from—it seems—the rest of the world; and peaks that you can easily climb to enjoy breathtaking panoramas of the main range.

The natural life of the Pyrenees is something that cannot fail to impress. Although the rarities and specialities—such as brown bear, bearded vulture, or lynx—may get mentioned most (and it is nice to know they are there), it is the marvellous displays of flowers, and the sheer abundance of things that will impress most visitors. There are flowers, butterflies and birds everywhere, and some of the displays of mountain plants are among the best to be seen anywhere in Europe. Hardly an hour—let alone a day—passes without an eagle, kite or vulture gliding overhead, and the other bird life is very rich too.

For the historian, the Pyrenees are fascinating, both as a barrier and a melting-pot, and there is much history to be read in the passes and villages of the mountains. The architecture reflects the religious and military history of the area, with forts, fortified churches, ruined castles, abbeys and monasteries, together with a fine series of different local styles of domestic houses, many of them very old.

However you decide to travel in the Pyrenees, you are unlikely to face any particular difficulties. The roads are generally good, especially on the French side, and most well-known sites can be reached by road (though, thank goodness, there are not yet roads everywhere, and many areas are totally unspoilt).

Walking is an ideal way to see the mountains, and the walker is well catered for, with way-marked routes, refuges and good trails, though

again it is easy to get off the beaten track and be alone if you feel like it.

The Pyrenees offer something for almost every visitor (they even have magnificent beaches, on two seas, at either end!), yet they remain reasonably unspoilt, and busy only in high summer. We attempt in the following pages to summarize some of the attractions and possibilities of the area, and to explain some of the underlying reasons for its special nature.

1. An imposing Basque farmhouse, with its winter woodpile, in Garralda, a village in the Navarra province of Spain.

CHAPTER TWO

The Pyrenees

The Pyrenees are one of Europe's import- ant mountain ranges. Although small compared with the Himalayas, Andes, Rockies or other major ranges, their significance within Europe is considerable. They stretch in an unbroken chain from the Atlantic to the Mediterranean, cutting off the Iberian peninsula from the rest of Europe like a vast wall, several thousand metres in height, nearly 450 kilometres (280 miles) long, and tens of kilometres wide.

It is sometimes said that 'Africa begins at the Pyrenees'. Whilst it is obviously not true in any literal sense, it does reflect the fact that the Pyrenees are, and especially have been, more of a physical, social and climatic barrier than the few kilometres of sea that separate southern Spain from Africa. The Moorish, Islamic influence on southern Europe virtually stops at the southern side of the Pyrenees, so the statement has some accuracy in that respect. Equally, the climate changes dramatically at the Pyrenees, with the northern, French slopes receiving considerable quantities of rain from north-westerly winds off the Atlantic, while the southern slopes are amongst the driest parts of Europe.

Finally, the terrain changes dramatically too, with the Pyrenees marking the sudden switch from the gentle plains of south-west France to the rugged, convoluted ranges of Spain. The Pyrenees are also, of course, an international boundary, though strangely enough they do not form quite such a clear-cut linguistic and ethnic boundary, as we shall see later.

THE EXTENT OF THE PYRENEES

The area generally known as the Pyrenees covers around 40,000 sq km (c. 15,000 sq miles), as measured on the map rather than the ground, where the area would be much greater. The international boundary between France and Spain runs roughly along the main ridge, but in places there is no clear main ridge, and in other areas the boundary ignores the main peaks and deviates unexpectedly. Andorra, the third Pyre- nean country, lies on the southern slopes, more Spanish than French.

On the French side, the edges of the Pyrenees are relatively clear-cut, as the ground rises steeply from the lowlands without the complica- tion of parallel ridges or high plateaux. The southern side of the ridge is much more complex, though, as the Pyrenees merge southwards into a complex of other sierras which stretch away southwards into Spain. Some, such as the Sierra del Cadi, can safely be included in the Pyrenees, while others cannot. On average, the Pyrenees are roughly 80–90 km (c. 50–55 miles) across, from north to south.

2. The village of Riglos (Spain) is dwarfed by the rose-coloured 'pudding stone' cliffs above it.

THE FORMATION OF THE PYRENEES

The Pyrenees are such a dramatic and clear-cut range, at least from the French side, that they immediately prompt the question, 'Why are they there?' The answer is not completely straightforward, of course, but it can be summarized.

The surface of the Earth is in a constant state of change. It has gradually been appreciated over the last few decades that the continents of the Earth are actually moving around (i.e. the modern expression of the old theory of 'continental drift'). In fact, it is not just continents that are moving, but whole areas of the Earth's surface called plates, some of which have continents, some of which do not. Where these plates meet, and one slides under the other, tremendous pressures result, and these boundaries are often the areas of greatest mountain-building activity; in terms of the size of the whole Earth, only tiny folds are being produced, no more in scale than the wrinkles on the skin of an orange. But to humans, the results are spectacular in the extreme, taking the surface of the Earth up to altitudes where the climate is considerably colder, and where snow is frequent.

The Pyrenees were formed in two main stages: by the collision of the Iberian plate with the European one, causing the dramatic buckling of Spain and the raising of its surface, and by the particular raising of the Pyrenees at the junction. The last major period of Pyrenean mountain building was during the Alpine orogeny—when the Alps were being formed—about 30 million years ago.

Once the surface has been buckled up into mountains—a process which itself takes millions of years—erosion begins to shape the range. The older the mountains are, the more rounded they are in outline (and generally, the lower they are), as in the Pennines in northern England. Relatively new mountains, like the Pyrenees, are still suffering tremendous erosion, which produces dramatic, jagged peaks, much

bare rock, and the familiar mountainous outlines that we see today.

In addition to the normal erosive processes of rain, wind, frost and so on, the Pyrenees, in common with many other mountain ranges, have been glaciated in the past. The Earth has suffered a number of ice ages, or glacial periods, in recent times, of which the most recent ended only about 10–12,000 years ago. During these periods, when the climate was much colder, snow accumulated in areas like the Pyrenees at a rate greater than that at which it melted, giving rise to glaciers flowing outwards from a great ice sheet, rather like Iceland today. The glaciers had tremendous erosive force, gouging out valleys and cutting back into peaks, such that they could be said to have shaped the Pyrenees into their present form. You can recognize a glaciated valley because it is U-shaped in profile, with a curved floor, and valleys often have steep cliffs at their heads (usually with a lake) where the glacier cut back into the mountain. Such glaciated valley heads are known as cirques on the French side, and circos on the Spanish side, and excellent examples occur at Gavarnie, Troumouse, and upper Ordesa. You can usually pick out the furthest downwards extent of the glacier by the marked change from the broad, U-shaped upper valley, to the narrow, V-shaped valley lower down, where only the rivers have eroded it. Often there is a marked hill at this point, comprising the remains of the debris brought down and deposited by the glacier—called its terminal moraine.

PYRENEAN WEATHER

Like most mountain ranges of any height, the Pyrenees can be said to make their own weather. However, not all parts of the range make the same weather, and the climate in the Pyrenees varies according to the aspect, proximity to the Atlantic or Mediterranean, and the heights of the peaks.

As a general rule, mountains are wetter and

snowier than the surrounding lowlands, as any moist air moving into the area is forced to rise by the mountains and its moisture load is precipitated as rain or snow. The amount of rain or snow, however, depends on the character of the air reaching the mountains in the first place. Mountains in a continually moist air stream are exceptionally wet, while mountains in a dry air stream can remain quite dry. In the Pyrenees, there is a little of everything.

The two main trends in the Pyrenees are a reduction in wetness from west to east, and a difference between the northern side and the drier, southern, Spanish side. The western end of the Pyrenees reaches the Atlantic Ocean at St Jean de Luz, or thereabouts, at the south-eastern

3. South of the central Pyrenees, in Spain, the countryside is dry and barren, as here, in the Río Isábena valley.

corner of the Bay of Biscay. This is an area of westerly, moisture-laden winds brought in by depressions from the Atlantic, and as soon as they hit the Pyrenees they rise and precipitate their rainfall. Thus the western end of the Pyrenees is green and well-watered, though it is by no means wet all the time.

As this damper air moves westwards along the range it loses its effect, so there is a progressive reduction in rainfall along the range towards the east. At the same time, the eastern end of the Pyrenees reaches the Mediterranean Sea at

Banyuls, or thereabouts; the Mediterranean, as is well known, has very dry summers under a high-pressure weather system, and the effect of this extends westwards along the range. Thus the eastern end has a dry summer climate. In winter the pattern is much more variable, as the Mediterranean weather becomes much more unsettled, and regular rain can be expected from October to April, with relatively more precipitation, usually as snow, in the mountains.

South of the range, on the Spanish side, the pattern is rather different. Much of the rain-bearing wind originates from north of the range, so the south-facing valleys lie in the rain-shadow of the Pyrenees themselves, at least where they are high enough to have this effect. However, winters in Spain are unsettled, and considerable rain may fall there, but the Pyrenees are protected somewhat from rain from the south by subsidiary ranges stretching away into Spain. The net effect of all this is that the western Spanish Pyrenees are damp, receiving rainy winds direct from the Atlantic, and getting little protection from north-westerlies as the peaks are lower here; the central Spanish Pyrenees, in the rain-shadow of the highest peaks, and protected by lower ranges to the south, are dry for much of the year; whilst at the eastern end there is no great difference between the north and south sides, with the Spanish side being slightly drier.

To emphasize the difference between the two ends of the Pyrenees, the western end is one of the wettest regions of France, with around 200 wet days per year, while the eastern end is the driest part of France! Between these two extremes, there is a vast range of microclimates along the general trends outlined. Thunderstorms are frequent, especially in summer, just to complicate the picture, and it is often said that there is a storm every four to five days in high summer. Although the pattern is not really so

4. The Ordesa National Park (Spain) is notable, amongst other things, for its waterfalls, cascading over a series of glacial cliffs and geological features.

exact, thunderstorms do occur often in warm, humid weather.

Snow falls, variably, throughout the range, and all the peaks become white-capped during the winter. Snow falls, on average, on 118 days per year at the top of the Pic du Midi de Bigorre (2865 m; 9400 ft), where there is an observatory and weather station. In most years, snowfields persist throughout the year on the highest peaks and north-facing slopes, though the extent depends on the depth of the winter snowfall and the warmth of the summer. Recently there have been several dry hot years, though in 1988 frequent rain and snow was experienced through the French Pyrenees right up to early July, to be followed by a dry warm winter, and a hot dry summer.

PEAKS AND VALLEYS

The Pyrenees are far from being an even wall of roughly equal height throughout their length. There are very definite changes along the length of the chain, which relate clearly to the degree of impassability and the amount of social interchange that has taken place.

The western end of the Pyrenees is Basque country. Here, the mountains are lower, more rounded, and greener. For much of the extreme west, there is really no physical barrier at all between Spain and France, and the Basque country extends without great change from Spain into France (except that French Basques seem to be rather more prosperous than Spanish ones). The higher peaks of the western end are often barely over 1000 m (3281 ft), and the first mountains of any real height are not reached until the cluster of peaks around the Pic d'Anie (2504 m; 8215 ft), towering above the Vallee d'Aspe, on the French side.

From here eastwards, the high Pyrenees begin, with the Pic du Midi d'Ossau (an exceptionally beautiful mountain at 2884 m; 9462 ft), Monte Perdido (the 'Lost Mountain', in Spain, at 3355m; 11,007 ft), Pic du Midi de Bigorre, (with its extraordinary astronomical observatory, at 2865 m; 9400 ft), and, highest of them all, Pico d'Aneto, in Spain (3404 m; 11,168 ft). The mountains are by no means a single jagged wall here either; for example, the Pic du Midi de Bigorre, which is no small mountain, lies about 25 km (15 miles) in a direct line north of the high peaks on the Spanish border; and the mountains extend well beyond the border to the south. In fact, though these peaks are of considerable height, they do not include the highest peaks in their respective countries. France has higher mountains in the Alps, whilst the highest mountain on mainland Spain is Mulhacen, in the Sierra Nevada, at 3482 m (11,424 ft); and the highest on Spanish territory is Mt Teide, on Tenerife (3710 m; 12,172 ft).

In this central area, the high peaks are simply too numerous to mention individually, and quite a number exceed 3000 m (9800 ft). Eastwards, though, the average height begins to fall again, and the Pic du Canigou, between Prades and Prat-de-Mollo, stands out as a high mountain at 2784 m (9134 ft). It is the last great eastern outpost of the Pyrenees and it dominates the landscape of this part of France.

The relative ease with which the Pyrenees can be crossed at the eastern end, as at the western end, has allowed a unified culture to develop which spreads across, and takes little note of, the international boundaries. Like the Basques, the Catalans inhabit an area that straddles France and Spain, with the Pyrenees running through it. Such a situation could not happen in the central Pyrenees, where individual adjacent valleys are often isolated from each other, let alone the opposite sides of the range. Until recent road developments, passes in the central area were impassable for much of the year, allowing little social interchange of any significance.

When to go to the Pyrenees

The Pyrenees can, of course, be visited at any time of the year, within the limits imposed by the weather conditions, but some periods are better

than others for different purposes.

Spring begins in April, at least in the lower areas, and this is a marvellous time to visit for clear views, early flowers, snow-covered mountains and beautifully quiet roads. Major roads are open, but many minor roads may still be blocked at altitude. The weather is mixed, with everything from warm sun to snow, though always likely to be cold at night.

May and June are a perfect time to be in the Pyrenees, with masses of flowers and birds but few tourists. Weather is still mixed, but can be very warm, and higher roads may be blocked until well into June. Camping is likely to be limited, until the first hay is cut. Most climbers avoid spring and early summer because of the avalanche danger.

July and August are very busy and access to the high tops is at its easiest. All facilities are working, or possibly overworked, and traffic jams are possible at peak times. The weather is at its most settled.

Autumn is overlooked as a time to visit the Pyrenees, though it can be a good one. The weather is unpredictable from October onwards, but is marvellous if you are lucky. A new range of flowers appears, including crocuses and their relatives, and beautiful autumn colours gradually develop. After mid-September, the roads become very quiet, yet most hotels, etc., are still open. The western end of the range can be very rainy, and some rain is likely everywhere from October onwards.

From December onwards, things get difficult. Snow falls regularly, and passes become blocked, whilst few facilities are open. The skiing season starts a little later, with the peak period around mid-February to March. At this time the roads to ski resorts are open, and many

5. The Pic du Midi de Bigorre (2865m; 9400 ft) is a high peak, isolated from the main range on the French side of the Pyrenees, topped by an observatory and TV mast.

hotels are open, so it can be a time for a winter visit without the intention of skiing. There is usually plenty of sun, though it is cold. Late winter is a good time for canoeing or river rafting, making use of the high water levels. Many climbers also visit in winter, specifically for the tough ice and snow climbing.

6. *The high Pyrenees abound with lakes; both natural glacial and artificial. This photograph shows the Lac d'Oredon in the French Pyrenees.*

CHAPTER THREE

The History of the Pyrenees

Any large mountain range poses a barrier to communication between peoples, and the Pyrenees, seeming to stretch like a huge wall from the Atlantic to the Mediterranean, has done this very effectively. A closer look will show that the Pyrenees are a mountain system, rather than a single range whose watershed stretches its whole length. In fact there are two mountain lines with a gap between them (neither of them running true east to west), so that in the Val d'Aran there is a part of Spain that geographically belongs in France. In the latter part of the twentieth century we take for granted the ability to travel easily, yet less than a hundred years ago people would have had to have very good reason to make the effort to negotiate this mountain chain. In fact, on the Spanish side the valleys are surrounded by hills so high that they are virtually inaccessible. This allowed the people of each to develop and preserve their own dialect and customs. Of course, the ambitions of conquering armies tend to ignore obstacles like mountains, but ordinary folk, intent on living their lives, have lived in separate communities on either side of the Pyrenees for many centuries. The building of tunnels and opening of passes has meant a degree of migration either side and it comes as quite a surprise to find that in Spanish towns some miles away from the border French is widely spoken as a second language and the Franc is an accepted, albeit unofficial, currency in shops.

In strict geographical terms the area constituting the Pyrenees is fairly easy to define as the dividing line between France and Spain. Yet culturally and linguistically it is diverse, and this has led to a complicated and sometimes turbulent history. Such diversity is further emphasized in the western and eastern sectors, where national borders are very definitely not the same as cultural divides. At either end of the gigantic Pyrenean barrier, where the mountains fall towards the coast, it has always been easier to travel from France into Spain. For example, in spite of national boundaries, easy mountain passes meant that members of the Basque nation could keep in contact with one another and preserve their cultural identity. Inevitably, the recognized national divisions are a bone of contention for two peoples, Basques in the west and Catalans in the east, with languages of their own and fierce nationalistic pride voiced by strong political movements intent on securing a separate identity for Basques and Catalans alike.

PREHISTORY AND THE ANCIENT PERIOD

Pyrenean culture is very old, as extensive cave drawings in Niaux and Bédeilhac reveal. These rival, in fact, the far more famous drawings in the caves at Lascaux in the Dordogne, which are now closed to public view.

At Bédeilhac the cave is so vast that it was used as an aircraft factory by the Germans during

their Second World War occupation of the region, and it features a stalagmite of enormous girth as well as wall and floor paintings from the Magdalenian period. The finest and most extensive cave art, however, is to be found at Niaux, to which entrance is gained from a hillside off the road to Vicdessos 4 km (2¼ miles) south-east of Tarascon. The entrance was made recently and replaces the original opening. Numbers of entrants are restricted. Advance booking has to be made so that the paintings can remain open to public view without deteriorating due to heat and pollution, as they did at Lascaux.

7. The monastery at Roncesvalles (Roncevaux), situated on a low pass in the western Pyrenees, is at the site of numerous historic events.

The third century BC

In the year 281 BC Carthage's most capable commander, Hannibal Barca, was in Spain protecting Carthaginian interests there against the energetic empire-building of the Romans. Although Carthage was the older power in the Mediterranean, with trading posts all around the seacoasts, the Roman state was young, ambitious and not readily disposed to letting anyone or anything stand in the way of expansion.

War broke out and Hannibal expected a Roman army to be despatched to Spain. He therefore crossed the Ebro from Cartagena ('New Carthage') in Spain with a force of 100,000 men and some 40 elephants to meet them in Catalonia. Any resistance from northern tribes between the Pyrenees and the Ebro was subdued by the end of June in that year and Hannibal waited—but in vain. Roman attentions had been turned towards a rebellion by Celts in northern Italy and Scipio's legions destined for Spain were diverted to quash it. Hannibal realized by September that the adversary was not coming to him and so, reducing his force to 50,000 infantry, 9000 cavalry and 37 elephants, he prepared them to march into Italy, strike suddenly against the Romans and convert the various tribes to his side.

This was the force that crossed the Pyrenees at Le Perthus and made first camp at Elne (Illiberis) on the far side. Although he won over a coalition of Gallic tribes near Perpignan, who were preparing to block his advance, Hannibal was ultimately defeated and the Roman Empire expanded throughout southern Gaul and Spain.

THE MEDIEVAL PERIOD

The ninth century AD

The people of the Pyrenees played a vital part in the lengthy struggle to keep the Muslim Moors first at bay and then out of Spain entirely.

The Spanish Marches (the border between Christian France and Muslim Spain) lay along the Pyrenean range and the constant efforts of the French to repulse the Paynim hordes gave rise to many works of literature. Perhaps the best known is the *Chanson de Roland* which tells of Charlemagne's general, Roland, and his death at the pass of Roncevalles (Roncevaux in modern French). Composed some 300 years after the event, it tells of the valiant efforts of a small group of Christian knights against the Saracens. Roland and his friend Oliver, both Paladins (peers of Charlemagne's court), were at the centre of the action. Harsh reality takes the romance out of the tale because it was a Basque, not a Saracen army, that ambushed Charlemagne's troops and caused the humiliation, while Roland, an obscure governor of Brittany seems to have been elevated to imperial favourite by the device of 'poetic licence'.

Apart from the odd skirmish this was the only resounding defeat of Charlemagne's campaigns and Christianity prevailed in the region. Many churches and monasteries were built during the eleventh and twelfth centuries in the different Pyrenean regions, thus helping to give a degree of cultural unity to an otherwise diverse people.

The twelfth and thirteenth centuries

This period saw the growth of Bastides—new towns built in rectangular patterns of intersecting streets, sometimes with generously proportioned squares with arcaded walks (*cornières*) in their centres. The principle streets in these grid systems were called *carreyous* and these were connected by alleys (*androjust*). A number of such towns (e.g. Labastide-Clairence, Mirepoix, Montréjeau) still exist in the Pyrenees, nearly all of them revealing evidence of the strictly geometric 'town planning' obviously in vogue in medieval times.

The Catharists (1140–1244)

Catharism was not originally French, but spread to southern France from Bulgaria and the gnostic heresy of the Bogomils.

The name means 'the pure ones' and although no proper record of the Cathar doctrine survived it seems that the seriousness of purpose of the sect in an age of Catholic decadence attracted converts and led to it becoming the alternative church in southern France after 1150. The Catholic Church of the time had become corrupt and materialistic with bishops ready to take bribes and keep mistresses as a matter of course.

8. The old twelfth-century chapel at Roncesvalles.

The Cathars did not alienate ordinary people, but spoke to them in *langue d'oc*, their own language, which was probably one good reason for their appeal.

The Cathars were dualists, believing that the forces for Good and Evil competed on equal terms in the world, but that the material world was the Devil's creation. Men and women, as material beings, were thus, from birth, evil, but God had provided them with souls, so they could be saved through the spiritual side of their being. To them the Old Testament, Mass, burial in consecrated ground, prayers for the dead and marriage were the work of the evil one and they rejected all these institutions outright. They had no doubt that it was the Catholic Church and not the Catharist movement which was heretical.

However, open Catharist opposition to papal institutions became tainted with political overtones: these were times when the feudal lords of Languedoc were not yet under the authority of the French Crown. This led to violent reprisals from Rome, and the armies of Pope Innocent III, aided by the apparatus of the Inquisition, hunted down Catharists.

The strength of Catharist belief and the widespread appeal of their faith meant that they were not easily silenced. Persecution started in

earnest in 1208 with the declaration of a papal crusade by Innocent III. The 'successes' of this venture included the sacking of Béziers in 1209 and the siege and capture of the town of Lavaur near Toulouse in 1211. In Lavaur some 400 Cathars were captured and burned alive. In the unhappy history of these devout people the most noted centre of defiance was the castle of Montségur where, in 1244, after a siege of ten months, 200 Cathars plus 150 soldiers and their families were eventually overcome. The terms of surrender were generous but the Cathars refused

to recant and were led down the mountain from the castle to be burned to death.

The fourteenth and fifteenth centuries

These were generally years of war and famine for the Pyrenees, although fishing fleets became

9. The ruined Cathar stronghold castle at Peyrepertouse, on the edge of the French Pyrenees.

important to the economic welfare of the Basque peoples. It is alleged that Basques were sailing up the Saint Lawrence River in Canada and along the coasts of Labrador, Greenland and Hudson's Bay as early as the thirteenth century. And a regular whaling fleet was supposedly operating off Greenland in 1412!

THE EARLY MODERN AND MODERN PERIODS

In the sixteenth century the *Edict of Villiers-Cotterets* imposed French as the judicial language.

The seventeenth century

Wars between France and Spain over the Pyrenean region ended in 1659 with the *Treaty of the Pyrenees*, which allotted areas along the Pyrenean divide to one or another of the countries concerned.

Rousillon and Cerdagne became French, which, given their geographic position is unsurprising. More bizarre was the decision (still adhered to today with distinct advantages for the tourist!) that Llivia in Cerdagne should belong to Spain. The formation of this Spanish enclave in France came about as a result of 'sleight of hand' on the part of Spanish diplomats negotiating the terms of the treaty. In order to preserve ready access to Roussillon, Cardinal Mazarin insisted that the French should have control over all the villages along the route over the Col de Puymorens and thence to Perpignan. The Spaniards were happy that the uppermost reaches of the River Segré should be regarded as French but Llivia was not a village. Indeed, the inhabitants of Llivia were insistent that it was a town, with a charter, and had been capital of Cerdagne as Julia Llivia in Roman times. It was granted the status of a temporary Spanish enclave and it has remained a part of Spain ever since.

The eighteenth century to the present

The end of this century saw the first real Pyrenean 'tourist', enthusing over the region and leading the way to later developments. Between 1787 and 1810 Raymond de Carbonnières made

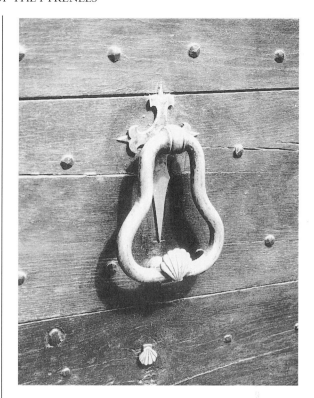

10. *Cockleshells, the symbol of pilgrims travelling to Compostella, still adorn a few buildings in St Jean Pied-de-Port.*

the ascent of the Pic de Bigorre 35 times, and in 1789 his work *Voyages dans les Pyrénées* was published.

Nineteenth and twentieth century trends have reinforced the attraction of the Pyrenees as a tourist region, particularly with the establishment of resorts where the effects of thermal springs could be enjoyed.

Both in the Catalan region of the east and, more heatedly, in the Basque regions the urge for political autonomy has often been violently expressed—more so on the Spanish than on the French side. Indeed, the modern Basque insistence on 'Enskadi Bat', 'Basques United', reminds us forcibly that this area has a history all its own, independent of French or Spanish history. The Pyrenean people are, it would seem, Pyrenean first and French or Spanish second.

BASQUE HISTORY

The highlands and foothills of the western Pyrenees were inhabited from very early times by the enigmatic Vascones, ancestors of the present day Basques and the Gascons. Little is known of the origin of the Vascones other than that they were probably one of the pre-Celtic Iberian tribes already well-established when the Visigoths came into Spain from northern Europe in the fifth century AD. The decline of Roman rule allowed tribes on the edges of the former empire

11. The French Basque town of St Jean Pied-de-Port derives its name from its position astride the pilgrim route over the pass into Spain and on to Compostella.

to become independent. Most of these tribes had presented little opposition to the advancing Visigoths. The Vascones, however, had successfully resisted Celts and Romans, and after initial skirmishes they were left well alone. Invading Moors in the eighth century forced the Vascones back into the highlands which now comprise the French and Spanish Basque regions and the province of Navarre. Here, virtually isolated, they maintained racial purity alongside their customs and language.

Charlemagne's campaign south of the Pyrenees pushed the Moors out of Pamplona, destroying much of the city in the process. The Vascones, considering all invaders alike, attacked Charlemagne's rearguard and killed Roland at the pass of Roncevalles. The same pass was part of the pilgrim route to the Shrine of St James at Santiago de Compostela, and the highland Basques, regarding the pilgrims as just another source of income, robbed them for many years.

The other inhabitants of Navarre established a kingdom in the ninth century, and in the eleventh century, under Sancho the Great, its influence extended well beyond its territorial boundaries as he sought to unify all of Spain under Christian rule. Even with these efforts the Basques remained isolated in the highlands. When Spain was divided by the Carlist wars of royal succession in the nineteenth century, the Basques supported the rebels, who lost. During the Spanish Civil War (1936–39) they were strongly fascist. Today the Basques are not completely integrated into Spanish politics and culture.

CATALAN HISTORY

Before the sixth century BC, an independent Catalonia had a profitable trading relationship with the Phoenicians and other Mediterranean seafarers. But its prosperity was increased by a series of invasions: Greek in the sixth century BC; Carthaginian in the third century BC and Roman in the second century BC. Catalonian commercial and political success then continued until the Moors invaded in the eighth century AD. The Christian population appealed to Charlemagne, who routed the Islamic forces and annexed the

region to his own empire.

Aragon, Catalonia's geographical neighbour on the eastern and central flanks of the Pyrenees, was established as an independent kingdom by Ramiro I Sanchez in 1035. In 1137, Petronila, the daughter of one of his successors, married the

Catalonian Count Ramón Berenguer, and the two states were brought under the same crown. This partnership lasted over 300 years, until 1479, and controlled Roussillon, Cerdaña (Cerdagne, east of Andorra), Valencia, Murcia, Sicily and the Balearic islands.

12. La Capella bridge, an ancient pack-horse-style bridge on an old drover's road through Espot, in the Spanish Pyrenees.

Despite political changes over the centuries, commercial ability has always enabled the Catalans to prosper, and their success has made their province the most prosperous in Spain. The Catalans, unlike the Basques, were pro-Republican during the Spanish Civil War and for them the period of Franco's rule meant the loss of what degree of independence they had.

Today, Catalonia comprises a total of some 26 provinces of which six lie within French territory. Throughout Roussillon the Catalan language is widely spoken by people of all ages, especially in rural districts; in fact it is the first language in Andorra as well as the official language of the administration in Barcelona. Today, that same Spanish city, not Paris or even Perpignan, is regarded as a 'capital' by the people of Roussillon and Catalan newspapers, television channels and schools are all to be found there.

ANDORRA

Andorra is the third Pyrenean country, one of the smallest countries in the world, squeezed between two of Europe's largest countries. Its separate existence is a peculiar anomaly, resulting from an agreement in 1278 under which the Bishop of Urgel (in Spain) and the Count of Foix (in France) agreed to equal stakes in Andorra, which became a principality. Subsequently, the French share passed to the French throne, was renounced by the French revolutionaries, but was re-assumed by Napoleon in 1806. The Andorrans petitioned the Emperor, because they feared that Spain would take them over wholly if France's rights remained renounced. The French rights are now vested in the President, while the Spanish ones remain with the Bishop of Urgel.

Today, Andorra is governed by an elected Parliament, dating from 1419, which meets in *La Casa de la Vall* in the capital, Andorra la Vella. Naturally enough, the country is part-French, part-Spanish in character (though rather more Spanish), with two currencies, a postal system run by both countries, and no taxes.

Its revenue comes largely from extensive sales of duty-free goods to Frenchmen and Spaniards, who drive into the principality for shopping sprees, and to fill the petrol tanks of their cars. It also caters for tourists and skiers, and grows tobacco for export.

LANGUAGE

In a technologically sophisticated world, there is growing interest in nationalist movements, particularly in Western Europe, where people draw deep comfort from the feeling of 'belonging' to an identifiable group with cultural traditions and perhaps a language of its own. As well as the official national languages of French and Spanish the Pyrenean peoples adhere to their ancient languages of *langue d'oc* and Catalan in the east and Basque in the west.

The terms *langue d'oc* for the language of the south and *langue d'oïl* for the French of the north reflect the different Roman accents when saying 'yes'. Not content with a single word they used *hoc ille*, meaning literally 'this that'. In the speech of the south this was shortened to 'oc' and in the north became *oïl*. The language itself evolved as a fusion of vulgar Latin and the speech used in southern Gaul before the Roman invasion. Even the everyday French of the region is peppered with words and phrases unique to the towns and villages of the Pyrenees, making conversation with locals something of a challenge for those who have learned textbook Parisian French!

The period of the troubadors spanned the eleventh to the thirteenth centuries, when long, lyrical love poems (*canso*) were written and performed at court. Their style of speech was elegant, if somewhat involved, and was much imitated in Italy and Germany as well as in northern France. An edict of 1539 proclaimed the language of the north as the official language for the whole country. Nevertheless, *langue d'oc* continued to be the language of the people until the early nineteenth century, when it was banned throughout schools by act of law. This law was

only repealed in 1951 and it very nearly destroyed the language, although it survived in everyday speech as patois. Today in the Pyrenees there has been a resurgence of interest in old Provençal—Langue d'Oc or Langue Occitane. In 1979, for example, it was offered as an option in the Baccalauréat (The French equivalent of Advanced Level) and drew over 6000 candidates from the youth of the region. The language, now often referred to as Occitan, is taught at Montpellier University.

Basque

Great mystery surrounds the origins of the Basque language, Euskara. It is a language so old and difficult that Basques maintain it must be learned from birth. Unfortunately, there is little in the way of a literature or history written in the language and reliance has had to be placed upon its strong oral tradition for clues as to its origin.

13. The Fort du Portalet, on the French side of the Col du Somport, symbolizes the military significance of the Pyrenean passes.

Some philologists have found similarities with Gaelic or Erse, others have claimed it to be a Phoenician dialect. In the nineteenth century George Borrow, with a certainty no other dared show, dismissed these ideas as nonsense and proposed that Basque was a dialect of Sanskrit— he believed, in fact, that all European dialects could be traced back to either Tibetan or Sanskrit—and thus that the Basques were of Asiatic origin.

Drs Saint-Paul and Eyquem of the Pasteur Institute in Paris have made extensive tests on Basque blood samples and concluded from the blood groups present that the Basques were the pure descendants of people who had occupied Europe in Paleolithic times and that their ancestors were the Franco-Cantabrians of the Old Stone Age whose stone tool assemblages have been found from Santander to the Dordogne. Basques claim a pedigree no other race in Europe can rival and that they are therefore the oldest inhabitants of Europe!

Basque spelling varies throughout the seven provinces and a few examples of common words are given below:

Egunon	Good day
Aratzalde-on	Good afternoon
Gabon	Good night
Ongi etorriak	Welcome
Plazer baduzu	Please
Eskarikasio	Thank you
Bai	No
Ez	Yes
Ardua	Wine
Uria	Water
Ogia	Bread
Hiria	Town
Itsasoa	Sea
Mendi	Mountain

Catalan

Catalan is an Indo-European language which originated from spoken Latin, as did the other Romance languages. In some ways it is a sort of cross between Spanish and French, and is not, as is Basque, impossible for the outsider to under-stand—especially when written down. The resemblance to Spanish is not as close as might be imagined and it sounds far more nasal when spoken. Also in contrast to Basque, there is a fine literary tradition, with many writers and poets of note, and its arts have consistently maintained a fresh identity, epitomized for example, by the surrealist painter Salvador Dali, a staunch Catalan.

Throughout Roussillon, signposts reveal the Catalan influence. Pronounciation is also dis-tinct, particularly with certain groups of letters:

CH is a hard sound like 'k'
G coming at the end of a word sounds like 'tch'
LL is pronounced as a 'y'
V is similar to 'b'
X becomes 'sh'

Distinctive words which appear frequently on maps include: *Estibe*—summer pasture; *Pla*—plateau or flat land; *Puig* or *Pech*—mountain peak and *Riu*—river.

34

CHAPTER FOUR

Pyrenean People and their Way of Life

Day-to-day life in the Pyrenees has always seemed to emphasize a distinct harmony between mankind and nature. Against a background of harsh wilderness and severe winters man has tried to use all available aspects of this existence and has made a successful attempt to exploit a difficult environment and survive from one millennium to the next. Life in the Pyrenees, as in mountain regions throughout the world, has depended on utilizing the land, and, broadly speaking, this allows us to divide the range into three sections according to the way they have been used: at the bottom lie the villages and settlements, where fertile land close to home is cultivated for a variety of vegetables, cereals and hay meadows in rotation; the upper lands provide grazing for cows, sheep and more unusually goats and horses; while the 'intermediate' zone has been largely exploited for cereal crops.

For countless centuries, in mountainous areas the world over, it has only been possible to look after the needs of domesticated animals by moving livestock from one region to another according to the season. Nepalese herders take their yaks up to over 5000 m (16,400 ft) in the Himalayas; Patagonians take their llamas and sheep high up into the mountain pastures of the Andes and the Bedouin tribesmen of Morocco lead their goats way up into the Atlas mountains. Transhumance, literally meaning 'across ground', was also once the way of life in the mountain regions of Europe. In recent years it has slowly become less common as people move from the harsh life of the mountains to the easier life of the cities. Widespread tourism in summer and winter provides an opportunity to make a good living in more comfortable and less demanding ways.

A mountain winter is definitely attractive to those with skis intent on a winter sports holiday and the *après ski* that goes hand in hand with it. Farmers, on the other hand, have to contend with direct sunlight reaching a village in a valley bottom for only a few hours a day for weeks on end. Snow covers the ground from November–December to April–May and animals have to shelter in large barns, feeding on the hay from the summer before.

When the snow melts, the manure from the barns is spread on the nearby hayfields, and cows and other animals are moved up the mountains as soon as possible to leave the fields in the valleys for crop cultivation. Many valleys are bordered by steep, tree-clothed hillsides and it is to the higher, flatter grassland areas called 'alps' that the animals are taken to graze. Small stone-built or wooden huts called *estives* provide a refuge for the members of the farmer's family who stay in the highlands to tend the animals, milking them and making cheese. Where transhumance is still practised today, animals are often moved by trucks. One consequence of this change has been the increase in animal respira-

tory diseases, particularly in sheep, since they have less time to make the acclimatization to greater altitude which the slower climb on the hoof provided in earlier times.

The attraction of regular wages at factories in towns and cities understandably lures the younger people away from the farms, and frequently the elderly are left to keep the farms going. Today a single person will often look after the animals of several owners, whereas in the past there was a great sense of community when sheep and shepherds from all the villages in a valley grazed their animals together on the same slopes. Several European governments have become concerned about the disappearance of transhumance and have tried to encourage its continuance by offering generous grants for each

14. The rolling, forested Basque country of the western Spanish Pyrenees, in Navarra province near Burguete.

15. A carpet-vendor in a Sunday street market in the eastern French Pyrenees.

animal moved onto the mountains. In Haut Languedoc to the north of Roussillon, for example, the Causses and Cevennes provide pasture lands for countless thousands of sheep and goats whose milk is used in the production of Roquefort cheese.

'Toussaint' (All Saint's Day, on the first of November) is traditionally the time when signs of winter force shepherds to gather their animals for the journey to lower pastures or to the abattoir. The animals, travelling in huge flocks,

16. Children cycling home with newly-cut stakes, near Pont de Suert, Spanish Pyrenees.

17. A massive flock of sheep (and a few goats) with four shepherds, in grassy pastures in the Val d'Aran, Spain. Such huge herds have a considerable effect on the vegetation.

wear coloured pompons for identification and are still driven along ancient traditional routes called *drailles*, some of which are like broad footpaths, whereas others have been turned into lanes or even roads through villages and towns by their use through the centuries.

In practical terms, a man who is away up a mountain for half the year is not always an attractive prospect for marriage and in some mountain regions many of the farmers were

18 Sheep grazing high stony pastures in late summer in the Val d'Aran.

traditionally bachelors, not so much by choice as from necessity.

Numerous other changes in long-held traditions have been forced by the movement of younger people to towns and also by differences in the style of farming. Sheep have often been replaced by cows; and single crops, instead of a variety, are often grown to exploit the terrain at different seasons.

Economic pressures from outside have sometimes forced changes which threaten the ecosystem of the region. For example, overgrazing to sustain larger flocks of animals has caused widespread destruction of traditional pastures and their famed floral display, especially on the French side. And to increase the yield of hay by securing two crops in a season, liquid manure is sprayed on the meadows which are then motor-mown. In the past, these fields would have been scythe-mown which, though admittedly laborious, allowed other plants to mature and their seeds to ripen. Thus, in mountain areas throughout Europe a sterile, continuous greenery has been steadily replacing the riotous displays of once-common meadow flowers and their clouds of attendant butterflies. In spite of the incessant demands of modern agriculture, however, some flower-filled meadows do still survive—and not only in the national parks of the Pyrenees.

Even if changes in a way of life mean that the *estives* have fallen into disrepair in many places, the remains of Pyrenean culture are fortunately still widely in evidence outside museums.

19 (following page). Hay-making time in autumn below the Pyrenean village of Valencia d'Aneu, Spain.

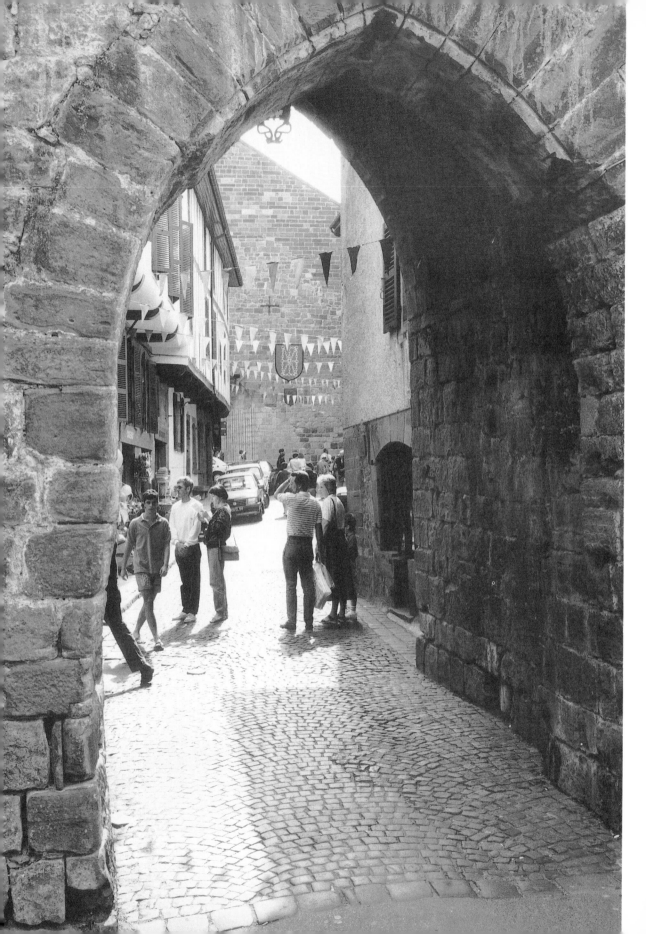

FESTIVALS

Virtually every small town has its traditional festival based on local saints' days, many of them coinciding with more ancient pagan celebrations of planting and harvesting, which the Christian Church has incorporated into its calendar. Some of the larger festivals are major annual events whose fame has become world-wide. This has certainly happened with the festival of San Fermin in Pamplona, an event which Ernest Hemingway is reputed never to have missed.

Spring festivals

These usually take the form of *carnivals*, such as those at Céret, Perpignan, Argelès and Vinça; or *bear festivals*, the traditional *Fêtes de l'Ours* held at Prats-de-Mollo and St Laurent-de-Cerdans.

Easter processions are a feature of life even in the smallest of towns in countries steeped in a tradition of Roman or Orthodox Catholicism. Religion for the Catalans has always been fervent, and the night of Good Friday is the time for the *Procession des Pénitents*, where black-robed figures form a procession through the streets of Arles-sur-Têt, Bouleternère and Collioure. In Perpignan *La Confrérie de la Sanche* (The Brotherhood of Blood) parades through the streets of the town in scarlet or black robes, hooded for the occasion, with slits for the eyes. Members carry carvings of wax or wood called *misteris*, and chant solemnly, providing a sinister, almost chilling spectacle—the more so when one realizes that the original role of these *Pénitents* was to minister to those condemned to death.

Easter Sunday is an altogether more joyous time, with Processions of the Resurrection and an excuse to parade through the streets of towns

20. A busy street in the old part of St Jean Pied-de-Port.

and villages throughout the region accompanied by the sounds of traditional chants.

Midsummer

Although much older than the Christian religion, the celebrations of Midsummer find a patron in St Jean, and bonfires are lit on Mt Canigou and other peaks as part of the *Fête de St Jean* on 23 June. At Amelies-les-Bains festivities and bonfires mark 24 and 25 June.

Summer festivals

In **Carcassonne** the month of July marks the *Festival de la Cité*, offering a varied programme of artistic, cultural and musical events to commemorate the city's involvement in the culture of the troubadours.

Pamplona's festival of San Fermin (7 July) has become far better known than the saint who gave his name to it. *Ferminus* was a local convert to Christianity in the third century AD who eventually became the first Bishop of Amiens. His festival has been celebrated on 7 July since 1591. It runs for seven days and accommodation in the city is full to overflowing. Participants dress in white with a red sash and a red scarf. Events during the week include 'running before the bull' and bullfights.

The second fortnight of July is *La Semaine Médiévale* in **Mirepoix**, a colourful celebration in which people dress in medieval costume and buildings are bedecked in the style of the times.

In **Bayonne** the first week in August sees annual festivities involving bullfighting, folk-dances, concerts and events on (and in!) the Adour river.

The Catalan *Festival de la Sardane* in **Céret** (last Sunday but one in August) is defined as 'a step dance where the step changes in the middle of the bar and the beat changes in the middle of a step'. The dance includes people called 'counters' whose role it is to keep the beat, and involves some 400 costumed dancers.

In **Carcassonne** the first two weeks in August are known as the *Journées Médiévales*, a mixed

Fronton Municipal de
Saint·Jean·Pied·de·Port

VENDREDI 8 SEPTEMBRE à 17 heures

GALA de
Pelote Basque
au Grand
CHISTERA

G. Garat
Recordman des titres nationaux (12 fois)
et son équipe
contre
SELECTION NAVARRAISE

16 h. Lever de Rideau avec les Jeunes Espoirs de l'Ecole de la Goïzeko

---

SAINT-JEAN-PIED-DE-PORT

AUX ARÈNES

TOUS LES LUNDIS
DE JUILLET
AOUT
et 4 SEPTEMBRE
à 21 h. 30

HAUTE ÉCOLE ANDALOUSE

GALA COMICO-TAURIN

Typical «landais» entertainment with Wild Cows

ÉCARTEURS · SAUTEURS · CLOWNS
JEUX D'AMATEURS · COURSE A LA COCARDE
PETITS VEAUX POUR LES ENFANTS

GANADERIA DARRITCHON
TEL. 59.29.66.37

En intermède :
DÉMONSTRATION
DE CHEVAUX ANDALOUS
HAUTE ÉCOLE ANDALOUSE

VACHETTES D'INTERVILLES

bag of medieval to modern-style entertainments, including archery, jousting and lightshows.

SPORTS

As a major tourist region the Pyrenees offer the chance to pursue a wide range of leisure activities and sports, including walking, climbing, cycling, canoeing, riding and skiing.

As a spectator sport for most visitors, rugby is well established on the French side of the Pyrenean chain, and has been played with considerable skill and enthusiasm since the earliest years of this century.

The Basque region offers the chance to watch *pelota*: the Basque national sport with a vocabulary of its own. It is played on a court, *fronton*, with a high back wall. Players, wearing a white and red sash, hurl a ball somewhat larger than a tennis ball at the end wall and catch it on the rebound in basket-shaped mittens called *chistera*, then hurl it back. There is also a version known as *main nue* (bare handed) and another called *trinquet* or *paleta*, which is played indoors.

Since 1900, the standard version of the game has been the *Jeu au Grand Chistera* which takes its name from the extended osier basket used on the hands of the players. The *grand jeu*, played with two teams of three players each, gained popularity largely through the skills of Joseph Apestuguy (1881–1950) who was known as 'Chiquito de Cambo'.

CUISINE

It is not realistic to speak generally of a 'Pyrenean Cuisine', for the people inhabiting each of

several different areas have their own culinary specialities. At the western and eastern ends of the range people make use of the plentiful supply of fish and other sea food. Thus, Basque dishes draw on a tremendous variety of fresh fish and are well worth attention. Catalan cooking likewise draws on fish but is also heavily influenced by Mediterranean tradition; and Catalan dishes, long respected throughout Spain, are now getting the wider attention they deserve in magazine articles and cookery books.

In the central Pyrenees, dishes have evolved using the meat of the animals kept locally. Hams and charcuterie in general are popular, as are stews of mutton and lamb cooked in various ways. Geese and ducks, force-fed three times a day on maize, produce the fatty livers that go into the production of pâté de foie gras. Hunting has remained a tradition in the Pyrenees and the prizes of *la chasse*, birds especially, feature in local dishes. Fresh trout from the mountain streams and lakes are also popular, and there are cheeses made from ewes' and cows' milk. Baking and deserts make ample use of local fruit – in particular the bilberries, *myrtilles*, picked high on the mountains, which appear in *tartes* (flans) of all sizes.

There follows a selection of regional Pyrenean dishes with summaries of their contents.

Basque cooking

1 *Bouillabaisse*—called *Ttoro* in Basque— depends for its success on six to eight different types of fish found off rocky coasts, such as wrasse, rascasse, red mullet, weaver, conger, bream, stargazer, bass, John Dory and monkfish. It is not, as is often supposed, a soup, but a complete meal: a composite soup plus fish dish!

The fish are scaled, gutted and cut into suitably-sized pieces, then added to a pan with finely chopped onions, the white parts of leeks, chopped tomatoes, garlic, parsley, orange peel, thyme, fennel, bay leaves, cloves, peppercorns and chilli. Olive oil is poured over them and sea salt sprinkled in before the whole lot is left to

21. Posters advertising pelota and comic bullfights in St Jean Pied-de-Port.

marinate for an hour. Finally, boiling water (or a mixture of white wine and water) is poured over the fish and the dish heated rapidly over a high flame for ten minutes or so to amalgamate the oil and water. To serve, the fish is lifted out on to a plate, the 'soup' poured into a tureen and the whole served with dried bread and a rouille of chilli, saffron and garlic.

2 *Piperade*—also known, with regional variations, in Provence, Turkey (as *Menemen*), Spain (as *Pisto*) and Tunisia (as *Chachouka*), and in Catalan as *Sainfana*—is a dish made with peppers, onions and tomatoes, cooked with egg beaten into the juices. It is somewhere in texture between an omelette and scrambled egg and delicious served with a green salad and crusty bread as a first course.

3 *Gateaux Basque*—cakes generally topped with liberal portions of cherry jam.

22. *A wrought-iron restaurant sign in the old fortified town of Villefranches de Conflent, eastern French Pyrenees.*

4 *Chipirones*—fresh baby squid, fried or cooked in their own ink—*chipirones en sua tinta*.

The ink sacks are carefully removed from tiny squid no bigger than a finger's length. They are cooked, inevitably, with tomatoes, garlic, onions and herbs (parsley), and the ink added shortly before serving.

5 Bayonne Ham—one of numerous local cured hams.

6 *Loukinkos*—garlic sausage.

Central region (Gascony, Béarn)

1 *Pâté de foie gras*—Goose and Duck Liver Paté.

2 Sheep's Milk Cheese—from Laruns or Sost, pressed into round 'cakes' and anything up to 5 kg (11 lb) in weight.

3 *La garbure*—soup of meat and vegetables.

Roussillon and Catalonia

With the Mediterranean close by it is hardly surprising that tomatoes, peppers, olive oil and garlic generously influence the dishes of the region. Distinctively piquant sauces are also a feature of the cuisine, a definite result of the influence of the region's long history of trade with the Levant. An unusual touch is the use of bitter oranges to flavour savory dishes.

1 *All y oli (Aïoli)*—a garlic mayonnaise made from olive oil, garlic and egg yolks.

2 *Anchoïade (Pa y all)*—Anchovy and garlic paste.

23. *A medieval church in Arties, Val d'Aran, now converted into a restaurant.*

3 *Barboufat*—a clear meat soup.

4 *Cargoulade*—snails barbecued on a fire of vine cuttings, served with *charcuterie*, bread and *all y oli* as a picnic dish.

5 *Cassoulet*—available in as many as three different versions as a thick stew based on white kidney beans and goose or duck liver with other meats.

6 *Civet*—a substantial stew, generally of game cooked with onions, red wine and the animal's own blood. Two well-known versions of the dish are *Civet de Lièvre* (hare) and *Civet de Sanglier* (wild boar).

7 *Civet de Langouste*—crayfish stewed with onions, garlic and herbs in white wine.

8 *L'Escalade*—a soup seasoned with thyme, garlic, oil and eggs.

9 *Friand de Fromage*—puff pastry filled with hot goat's cheese.

10 *Majado* (meaning something pounded)—a paste based on nuts (almonds, hazelnuts and pine kernels) and used to give consistency to other sauces and dishes.

11 *Moulade*—grilled mussels.

12 *Mouton à la Catalane*—mutton cooked in white wine together with ham, garlic and vegetables.

13 *Perdreau à la Catalane*—a stew of partridges with peppers and bitter oranges.

14 *Romesco*—a sauce made with hot red romesco peppers, hazelnuts, almonds and pimentos. This is the sauce that epitomizes Catalan cuisine.

15 *Salade Biquetoux*—a mixed salad served with Biquetoux, a goat's cheese.

16 *Saucisse à la Catalane*—spiced sausage slices fried with herbs, garlic and orange peel.

17 *Zarzuela, Bourride*—Catalan fish stews. As with *Bouillabaisse* the creation of the final dish is something of a work of art. Zarzuela depends more on shellfish and the result is a brightly coloured mix of shades of red and white touched with the yellow of saffron. Together with prawns, shrimps and lobster, squid and monk-fish are added for their firmness of flesh. In southern Spain grouper fish is also considered to be an essential ingredient.

24. *Speciality products from the Vallée des Aldudes, including red chilli peppers, outside a shop in the western French Pyrenees.*

WINES

The phylloxera epidemic of the last century had a devastating effect on the vineyards of the Basque region as well as on those in the rest of France. Viticulture continued in Europe by grafting phylloxera-free vines on to resistant American stock, but in the Basque region the grafted plants were never properly replanted, except in Irouléguy, a small hamlet at the foot of a hill. The only compensation for the wine-buff seems to be the abundance of large and small vineyards of the nearby Bordeaux region and the plethora of famous-name wines they produce.

To the south of the Basque region, through the Pyrenean foothills, lie the Rioja vineyards, home of the superb red and white wines of that name. Red wines from Navarre have only appeared in quantity on supermarket shelves in the past few years. The wine-drinking public has realized that though they may not rival the better Riojas they are nevertheless reliable in quality and an economical way of purchasing most enjoyable full-bodied red wines.

North-east of Pau and Tarbes, lying roughly between the Adour and Garonne rivers, is the region whose distilleries are entitled to produce Armagnac. Covering an area of some 35,000 hectares (c. 86,500 acres) it produces white wine of a fixed acidity, which is distilled to produce over eight million bottles of Armagnac in a season. It is exported world-wide.

The dry heat of the eastern Pyrenees, where they descend to the Mediterranean, provides ideal conditions for the production of some 55 million bottles of red wine per annum, of which over half are designated *Vin de Pays de Pyrenées-Orientales*. This label is used for the *département*, within which there are actually five zonal *vins de pays*, of which *Catalan*, resembling a light *Côtes de Roussillon* in its dusty, attractively fruity character, is the most important. The arid land suits the production of red wines best and the Carignon grape dominates the vineyards where this red wine is produced. Despite this,

about 1½ million bottles of white *vins de pays* are produced, of no special note, but enjoyable if drunk very young.

The sunny limestone hillsides of Roussillon and the Corbières, immediately to the north produce highly palatable wines—in particular, soft reds. From the Corbières, those based on the Carignon grape are almost dusty to the taste, but at the same time are sturdily fruity and best drunk young. *Fitou*, again mainly from the Carignon grape, was recognized as a special wine over 40 years ago and given the right to carry the designation *Appellation contrôlée*.

The stocking of *Corbières* and *Fitou* by large supermarket chains, at reasonable prices, has made these wines as familiar to the general wine-buying public as some of the Bordeaux wines. And although red wines certainly predominate, there are noteworthy whites such as a *Côtes du Roussillon* from the Macabeo grape and the deep gold *Muscat de Rivesaltes*.

Wine quality

France has a complex and almost foolproof method for ensuring the consistent quality and authenticity of its wines. It relies on the belief that the soil a vine grows in and the variety of the grape grown are of paramount importance to the final character and quality of a wine.

The basic wine is designated *Vin de Table*, literally table wine. Above this there are three levels of quality control. At the top of the list come wines bearing the *Appellation d'Origine Contrôlée* (Controlled Appelation of Origin, abbreviated AOC or simply AC). All the great 'classic' wines and most other top wines come into this category. Following these comes *Vin Délimité de Qualité Supérieure* (Delimited Wine of Superior Quality or VDQS), which can represent a sort of probationary phase before promotion to AC is considered. Finally, there is the *Vin de Pays* (Country Wine), which was created in 1968 to give a geographical identity and a yardstick of quality to wines previously only sold for blending. Supermarket shelves often have wines of good quality at reasonable prices bearing this label; in fact wines of the eastern Pyrenees are usually found in this category.

25. The western French Pyrenees are famous for cheeses and the wines of one area—Irouleguy.

CHAPTER FIVE

The Naturalist in the Pyrenees: vegetation and flowers

LANDSCAPE AND GEOLOGY

Stretching some 450 km (280 miles) from the Mediterranean to the Bay of Biscay, with a maximum width of 130 km (81 miles) and a central region that never falls below 1700 m (5580 ft) the Pyrenees present a formidable barrier to the movements of plants and animals. Although at first sight it appears to be a continuous 'wall', a closer look will show that the Pyrenees are a mountain system, with two mountain lines rather than a single range. Neither of these runs true east–west, and there is a gap between the two lines such that in the Val d'Aran there is a part of Spain that geographically belongs in France. The interior, in common with the Alps, tends to be composed of hard, crystalline rocks such as granites, schists and gneisses, which weather slowly. Outer bands are of sedimentary rocks with a predominance of limestones deposited in the Mesozoic and Tertiary ages which have eroded over the centuries.

High in the mountains, the presence of glacial lakes, U-shaped valleys and moraines indicates extensive glaciation during the ice ages, but today, in contrast with the Alps, there are no glaciers of any size.

The French and Spanish Pyrenees differ in appearance for a number of reasons, one of which is the way the northern slopes fall away steeply to the lower country of Aquitaine while the southern side falls, much more gently, in a series of parallel ridges to the flat plateau of the Ebro basin. The Ebro river itself is fed by water from the main range, which often has to flow parallel to the lower ranges before cutting abruptly through them in deep gorges.

The first of the parallel ridges belonging to the southern Pyrenees is composed of rocks formed during the Mesozoic, with much limestone in evidence; Tertiary marls and conglomerates characterize the middle range, with a return to Mesozoic formations in the sub-Pyrenean range which forms the southernmost ridge.

FLORA

Changes in Pyrenean topography, geology and climate from north to south also lead to considerable differences in vegetation. The French side is generally greener than the Spanish side, but many lush mountain pastures are overgrazed by large numbers of horses, sheep and cows capable of devouring anything of botanical note.

Left undisturbed, there would usually be a gradual succession of plant communities from grasslands to scrub to forest. Man's agricultural activities over the centuries have changed the face of the land, particularly in low-lying areas, and encouraged a diversity of vegetation. Small-scale agriculture has not created serious ecological problems, but when overgrazing and intensive cultivation become the norm whole plant communities begin to disappear.

Vegetation zones

Throughout the world, mountain vegetation falls into distinct zones, each recognizable by their characteristic plants. Exactly where these begin and end depends on where the mountains are, whether their aspect is northern or southern and what the soil is composed of. As a rough guideline, beginning at sea level, the altitude zones of the Pyrenees are as follows:

Littoral (coastal) zone	0–100 m (0–325 ft)
Lower hill zone	100–400 m (325–1300 ft)
Sub-montane (middle) zone	400–600 m (1300–1950 ft)
Montane zone	600–1400 m (1950–4600 ft)
Sub-Alpine zone	1400–2000 m (4600–6500 ft)
Alpine zone	2000–3500 m (6500–11,500 ft)

26. Recently-shorn sheep in the French Pyrenees, grazing in a pasture with wild daffodils, Pyrenean pansies, and other flowers.

It is not difficult to recognize these zones once their characteristic plants have been identified. An important start can be made by noting the trees present. For example, in the Montane zone beech is the dominant tree and it can grow densely on steep valley sides, where it is difficult to exploit. Ash, elm, sycamore, box, yew and evergreens can also be present in large numbers. Beech generally favours the warmer, drier regions on the south-facing mountain slopes,

whereas the silver fir grows where mists collect and tends to occupy the middle forest zones in the north-facing valleys of the Pyrenees.

At higher altitudes mountain pine becomes the dominant tree, and alpenrose (*Rhododendron ferrugineum*) and juniper form a dwarf-shrub layer which extends as a mountain 'scrub' above the tree line in the Sub-Alpine zone. The mountain pine forms forests up to 2400 m (8000 ft) in the Néouvielle Nature Reserve within the Pyrenees National Park and isolated trees occur up to an altitude of 2600 m (8500 ft), well into the Alpine zone.

On the drier, southern slopes of the Pyrenees Sub-Alpine vegetation often comprises a 'hedge-hog' zone of low, spiny shrubs which take on a dome shape to cope with heavy snow cover, strong winds, arid summers and a short growing period. Surprisingly, the pea family (*Leguminosae*) is well represented by spiny, intricately-

27. Pheasant's eye daffodils (Narcissus poeticus) dominating a mid-altitude meadow in spring in the French Pyrenees.

branched bushes with tiny leaves. Their isolation on high mountains for long periods has meant that some plant species have had time to evolve slowly and become subtly different from similar species elsewhere. In the Pyrenees there are a surprising number of plants found nowhere else in the world—some 180 endemic to the region—and even within the Pyrenees they can be confined to limited areas.

Vegetation in the true Alpine zone is sparse because conditions are so harsh, and the plants tend to favour habitats such as cliffs, gullies, crevices, screes, moraines, seepages and glacial lakes, where a thin soil can slowly accumulate and they can have a degree of protection. Many of the plants are perennials that form low cushions or rosettes, and their flowers tend to be large in comparison with the rest of the plant. By this means they are able to attract the relatively few insects at that altitude which might pollinate them. True Alpine plants survive in harsh conditions, protected by snow in winter and often shaded from the sun's full glare in summer.

Flowering Plant Communities

Although plants can be sorted out according to the altitude at which they grow, the divisions are very broad, because many mountain flowers are extremely particular in their requirements for survival. When hunting for specific plants a lot of time can be saved by learning to read some of the clues in the landscape. To understand why particular plants grow where they do there are a number of factors to take into account. The first of these is soil: the acidity (pH) is crucial to many plant species. Calcareous rocks (limestones and chalk) are distinctly alkaline and plants growing in the soils formed from these rocks are quite different from those where the rocks are siliceous (containing quartz and various silicates), such as granite, sandstone, schist and gneiss. Although siliceous rocks are more or less neutral in their acidity or alkalinity, soils formed from them will tend to be slightly acid because of the inclusion of decayed plant materials.

Another factor to consider is aspect. Whether a slope faces north or south makes a big difference to the amount of light the plants receive and, in the case of the Pyrenees, to the level of rainfall. The south-facing slopes are warmer and, because most of the rain falls on the north side, drier too.

Finally there is the question of the terrain itself. Rock faces can provide open exposure to the sun and shady crevices; stony slopes or screes look inhospitable but provide shelter and good drainage; in grassy areas the gradient of a slope can matter, as can the presence of long or short grass.

Some plants tolerate a wide range of conditions while others need more specific ones.

Without knowing the particular 'recipe' that suits a species it can be almost impossible to find it unless luck intervenes. After a short time, looking at and summing up a piece of ground becomes second nature: there is no mystique, just observation and practice.

Taking these various factors into account we can identify four quite different habitats in the Pyrenees, each of which offers a range of conditions for different plants. The overleaf diagrams show how this works in practice.

PYRENEAN SPECIALITIES

Alpine gardeners are familiar with a large number of attractive plants that carry the word *pyrenaica* as part of their scientific name. This is not always a watertight guarantee that the wild plant is restricted to the Pyrenees, but many of the more attractive species are.

One of the best known is the yellow Turk's cap lily (*Lilium pyrenaicum*), flowering in June or early July according to altitude, often with a backdrop of snow-capped mountains to add to its photogenic appearance.

Another example is the Pyrenean snake's head (*Fritillaria pyrenaica*), which has large bell-shaped flowers, coloured deep, brownish-purple with a few green marks on the outside. It flowers in mountain pastures, occasionally growing alongside a scarcer plant, the Pyrenean columbine (*Aquilegia pyrenaica*).

Limestone cliffs provide a home for the Pyrenean saxifrage (*Saxifraga longifolia*), which the plant hunter Reginald Farrer described as one of the 'grandest of the race' with its leaves forming a 'huge silver star-fish, rosette splayed against the cliffs', and flower spikes as 'regal fox-brush spires of white, standing stiffly straight from the face of the rock.'

28 (following page). An ancient lichen-covered beech forest high in the Ordesa valley, Spain.

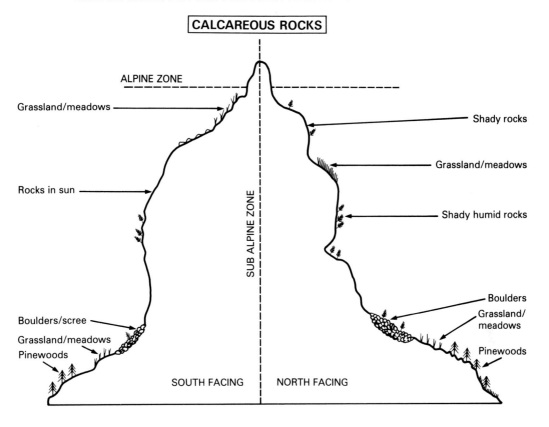

CALCAREOUS ROCKS

ALPINE ZONE

Grassland/meadows

Shady rocks

Rocks in sun

Grassland/meadows

Shady humid rocks

SUB ALPINE ZONE

Boulders/scree

Grassland/meadows

Pinewoods

Boulders

Grassland/meadows

Pinewoods

SOUTH FACING | NORTH FACING

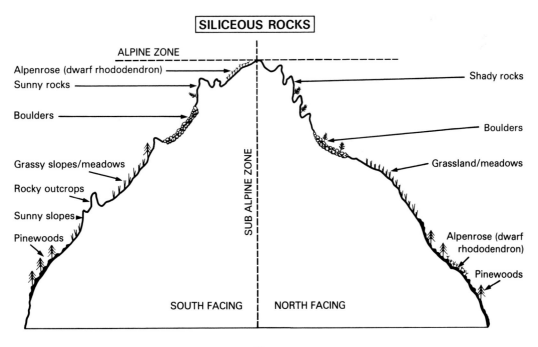

SILICEOUS ROCKS

ALPINE ZONE

Alpenrose (dwarf rhododendron)

Sunny rocks

Shady rocks

Boulders

Boulders

SUB ALPINE ZONE

Grassy slopes/meadows

Grassland/meadows

Rocky outcrops

Sunny slopes

Pinewoods

Alpenrose (dwarf rhododendron)

Pinewoods

SOUTH FACING | NORTH FACING

Shady crevices, usually, but not exclusively, on limestone, provide the favoured sites for the Pyrenean ramonda (*Ramonda myconii*), a very attractive member of the Gloxinia family with large blue-violet flowers and yellow anthers.

Androsaces are primrose relatives, at home on mountain heights. They form neat, flower-covered cushions and are great favourites of the Alpine gardener. They can be very particular in their growth requirements and three of those species that grow in the Pyrenees are endemics: *A. pyrenaica* (on granitic rocks and screes in the eastern region), *A. ciliata* (on limestone rocks and screes in the eastern region) and *A. cylindrica* (on limestone rocks in the Sub-Alpine zone of the central and eastern regions). The last two species are very rare in the wild and are better known as cultivated plants.

While the botanist and serious plant enthusiast can get great pleasure from finding a single rare plant, it is the floral displays in the Pyrenees, whether in spring, summer or autumn, that are a delight to any eye, and the justification for carrying good supplies of film.

When to go. This is not so easy to specify. If it is possible to talk about a 'typical year' then one can usually travel freely on the French side from mid June onwards: the flowers are at their best throughout June and July, depending when animals start to graze. In a late year the passes can be blocked by snow well into July, whereas September can sometimes provide displays of *Colchicums, Merenderas* and *Crocus*. Flowers on the Spanish side tend to be at their best some two to three weeks earlier than their counterparts on the French side, and the further east one is, the more advanced the flowering will be.

Where to go. One of the attractions of the Pyrenees is the ease with which one can get off the beaten track. The places below are only suggestions for starting points. It is a real pleasure to wander through an area surrounding oneself with high mountains, glorious flowers, butterflies and birds.

Western Pyrenees

Col du Somport

The main route from Pau into Spain passes over the Col du Somport, which is open most of the year, and is worth travelling towards the end of May for the displays of elder-flower orchid (*Dactylorhiza sambucina*) dotting the ground with magenta and yellow spikes between the snow patches. The slopes descending towards Jaca are worth searching for many of the western Pyrenean flowers, especially for the Pyrenean hyacinth (*Hyacinthus amethystinus*), a delicate china-blue bluebell.

East of Jaca, the going is more difficult on the C314 to Sabinánigo, but the reward is a drive up the Valle de Tena to Sallent for staggering views of the finest Pyrenean peaks: Pic du Midi d'Ossau (1884 m; 9462 ft), Pico Balaitus (3144 m; 10,315 ft) and Pic de Vignemale (3298 m; 10,820 ft). Flowers are to be found in a superb setting, including ramonda (*Ramonda myconi*), Pyrenean honeysuckle (*Lonicera pyrenaica*) and rock snapdragon (*Antirrhinum sempervirens*).

Ordesa

By turning east at Biescas on the road to Sallent one can travel via the Puerto de Cotefablo to Torla and the incomparable Parque Nacional de Ordesa. This is a wildlife showpiece, with flowers, butterflies, birds and larger animals in a breathtaking setting. There are numerous paths providing walks through unspoiled forests of beech, pine and silver fir that clothe the sides of the main valley of the Ordesa River.

The climb up past the waterfalls to the Alpine meadows at Soaso (2100 m; 6900 ft) brings the walker into a broad, U-shaped glaciated valley where the eye is dazzled by blue drifts of the Pyrenean hyacinth (*Hyacinthus amethystinus*), the white or pale pink of ashy cranesbill (*Geranium cinereum*) and deep magenta spikes of marsh orchids (*Dactylorhiza majalis*) together with extraordinary displays of rock-roses in many different colours.

Pic du Midi d'Ossau

In August when passes are open, the road beyond Sallent leads via the Col du Pourtalet to the east of the Pic du Midi d'Ossau and country where the spectacular Spanish iris (*Iris xiphioides*) grows in large numbers, its imposing flowers showing a deep purple against a rugged mountain backdrop.

Gavarnie and Gèdre

For the traveller anxious to escape from crowds Gavarnie suffers from its closeness to Lourdes and the fact that a detour there seems to be *de rigueur* for pilgrims. It is only by walking early in the day or late in the evening that one can selfishly enjoy the magnificent Cirque de Gavar-

29. *A montane hay meadow above Luchon comes into flower again after the final hay crop with a mass of purple autumn crocuses* (Colchicum autumnale) *in September.*

nie and the flowers that grow close to it. A footpath from the cirque leads up to the Brèche de Roland where endemic androsaces grow and from Gavarnie one can reach the Vallée d'Ossoue leading at its head to the glaciers of Vignemale. Pyrenean flowers abound and ramonda seems to cover the rocks in places.

Near Gèdre there is the Cirque de Troumouse, which is perhaps less impressive than that at Gavarnie. It lies at the head of the Val d'Héas, a valley full of wild flowers—the toll road through it represents a small sum of money well spent!

Central Pyrenees

Luchon

The spa town of Bagnères de Luchon provides a centre for a number of worthwhile excursions to search for Pyrenean wild flowers. The flowers of lower levels grow readily on the hillside leading to Superbagnères. The drive and then walk up to the Lac d'Oô offer the possibility of finding two endemics: ramonda (*Ramonda myconi*) and the pyrenean lily (*Lilium pyrenaicum*), as well as a chance to take in some superb scenery. After travelling from Luchon over the Col de Peyresourde one can take the route from Arreau to the lake of Cap de Long, looking down on the wooded Lac d'Orédon en route. In the stony ground and slopes around the lake grow Gentians (*Gentiana verna*), large butterwort (*Pinguicula grandiflora*) and the sweet-smelling garland flower (*Daphne cneorum*). For the more intrepid, with time to spare, the screes leading to the jagged peaks that form the amphitheatre around the lake are worth searching for cushion-forming Alpines.

Val d'Arán

The Val d'Arán can be reached from the Col du Portillon, about eight km (five miles) east of Luchon, from St Béat via the Garonne valley or from Lerida in the south. Because of a kink in the border it lies in Spain yet is on the northern slopes of the Pyrenees. Flowers are plentiful and varied, as the valley has both granitic and calcareous areas—in fact, soon after crossing the border one is aware of the comparative abundance of flowers on the Spanish side. Small walled villages are perched high up along the length of the valley and the adventurous can occasionally find negotiable tracks beyond them that take one through country full of flowers and butterflies. Pyrenean columbine (*Aquilegia pyrenaica*) Pyrenean fritillary (*Fritillaria pyrenaica*) and some unusual *Narcissi* are to be found here.

The Puerto de la Bonaigua (2072 m; 6798 ft), accessible from Salardu, is also well worth exploring for flowers growing between the snow patches in mid-June.

In autumn, with a final splash of colour before winter sets in, the Sub-Alpine turf is dotted with the magenta stars of merendera (*Merendera montana*) and leafless crocus (*Crocus nudiflorus*) with purple flowers carried on long, bare stems.

Eastern Pyrenees

Andorra

Almost immediately after leaving the unprepossessing frontier town of Pas de la Case on the climb to the Port d'Envalira (2407 m; 7897 ft) the path leading to a delightful lake, Étang de font-Nègre, takes one to Alpine flowers. Here grow pink primulas (*Primula elatior* and *P. integrifolia*), Alpine snowbells (*Soldanella alpina*) blue gentians (*Gentiana alpina, G. verna* and *G. pyrenaica*) and an abundance of the pale lemon Alpine pasque flower (*Pulsatilla alpina ssp. apiifolia*).

Beyond Port d'Envalira and its radio station lies Soldeu, a useful centre from which to search for wild flowers because of the Cap del Port above (with a fine display of Alpines in the short turf around its crags), and the Vallon d'Inclès below. Here, surrounded by high crags grow narcissus, iris, saxifrages, hepatica (*Hepatica nobilis*), rock jasmines (*Androsaces*) and an abundance of other flowers.

Col de Puymorens—Font-Romeau—Val d'Eyne

The N20 going east out of Andorra passes through an area around the Col de Puymorens (usually enveloped in cloud) rich in the wild

30. *Even the high-altitude forests are managed in France; in the Foret d'Issaux, these beeches have been coppiced and the silver fir trees selectively felled.*

flowers of the eastern Pyrenees. North of the Col is a marvellous lake-strewn area leading to the Pic Carlit, which can be approached from Mont-Louis by a narrow road to La Bouillouse, the largest of the lakes below the peak. For flowers and scenery it is a superb drive, with Pyrenean and St Bruno's lilies (*Paradisium liliastrum*) on wooded crags and Gentians and Crocuses around the lakes and streams above La Bouillouse.

By taking the road from Bourg-Madame to Olette access can be gained to the valleys that run due south of the road into the hills forming the frontier with Spain. The Val d'Eyne is quite outstanding for wild flowers, including Pyrenean lilies, Alpine aster (*Aster alpinus*), alpenrose (*Rhododendron ferrugineum*) and Pyrenean adonis (*Adonis pyrenaica*): the Val du Segré, entered via the Gorges du Segré near Llo, has an abundance of saxifrage and Pyrenean vetch (*Vicia pyrenaica*).

1   A refuge at Goriz (central Spanish Pyrenees),
capable of sleeping and feeding over 100 people.
There is a small weather station next to the refuge.

2   The extraordinary floral display in midsummer in
the higher parts of the Ordesa valley, with pink
rockroses in the foreground.

3   A late winter view of the developing ski resort and duty-free shopping area on the border between Andorra and France – Pas de la Casa. In summer, it looks most unattractive.

4   The small town of Gedre, in the central French Pyrenees, makes an excellent base for the National Park area. The high peaks above Gavarnie are visible behind.

5   The extraordinary rosettes and flowering spikes
of Pyrenean saxifrages, growing high on a cliff in
Ordesa valley. They flower once, after many years of
growing, then die.

6   The dramatic high cliff scenery in a side canyon in
the Ordesa National Park (over the page).

8   *An attractive triangular barn in high meadows above Gedre, central French Pyrenees.*

7   *The spring flowers start surprisingly early, even at high altitude. These April crocuses are in full flower in high Andorra, just as the snows melt from the pastures (previous page).*

9 A chamois, with its thick winter coat still noticeable, in high pastures in spring, just as the snow is melting.

10 The strikingly-coloured Merendera montana flowers fill many pastures at medium altitude on the Spanish side in autumn.

11   *The high border peak of Pui Pla (2825 m; 9263 ft) seen across Lake Ratera in the Aigues Tortes National Park.*

CHAPTER SIX

The Naturalist in the Pyrenees: animal and bird life

The Pyrenees are famous for their superb displays of flowers, and many visitors come almost entirely for this reason. Less well-known, but equally interesting and special, are the mammals, birds, amphibians, reptiles and invertebrates which collectively make up the exceptional Pyrenean fauna.

Most mountain ranges have a particularly interesting fauna. Mountains are almost invariably the last bastions against exploitation and development in populous countries, and many once widespread species are gradually forced back into the mountains, steadily retreating to the highest or wildest areas as the pressure increases. Thus, mountains are refuges for species now rare but once common, which are not really specialist mountain species at all. In addition to these, though, there are the specialized mountain species that have evolved particular adaptations to mountain life, and which may never have been more widespread. Such species often live at the highest levels.

The Pyrenees have a good measure of both groups, and their wonderful diversity of unspoiled habitats, their considerable altitude range, the variation in climate between north and south, and the relatively low degree of development and pressure, all make for a fascinating and diverse mixture of animal groups. Their isolation from the main groups of European mountains has also led to the evolution of a few Pyrenean specialities, as with the plants, such as the extraordinary Pyrenean Desman.

MAMMAL LIFE

Generally speaking, the casual tourist is unlikely to see much in the way of mammal life, apart from the occasional deer or squirrel. In the Pyrenees, though, your chances of seeing something in the way of mammals is greatly increased compared to the lowlands. For one thing, there are more species, and especially more large species; and secondly, more mammals remain active by day, instead of only appearing at night as most lowland mammals do.

Seeing mammals

Although mammals occur in abundance in the Pyrenees, few people catch more than an occasional fleeting and distant glimpse of them. There are, however, a few useful rules that can greatly improve your chances of getting close to wild animals.

1 Get up early or stay out late, or both. Many species are much more visible early in the morning or in the evening, by which time most people have left the mountains.

2 Do some research and find out what species are likely to occur where. In National Parks and reserves, try asking local rangers or wardens for more information.

3 Move quietly and unobtrusively. Noisy groups of people rarely see anything!

4 Use binoculars to scan ahead constantly, look at cliffs, check inaccessible areas, etc. It is amazing what you can pick up in this way.

5 If you are trying to get close to a particular group of animals, bear in mind that they are usually most sensitive to scent, so it is best to approach upwind where possible.

It is not possible to cover all Pyrenean mammals in a short chapter, so we have just picked out a few specialities, together with some of the most interesting and often-seen species.

Brown bear, *Ursus arctos*. A small population of the beautiful brown bear still occurs in the more forested areas of the western Pyrenees. The area is one of Europe's last refuges for this rare and declining species, though in 1979 there were reckoned to be less than 20 individuals in the Pyrenees, a number which offers little hope of long-term survival.

Pyrenean desman, *Galemys pyrenaicus*. The Pyrenean desman is an extraordinary creature, unlikely to be confused with anything else, if you should be lucky enough to see one! It is best described as an aquatic version of a mole (to which it is related) with a long snout, a long tail, and webbed hind feet. It occurs in and around mountain streams up to about 1200 m (3950 ft).

Numerous **bats** occur throughout the Pyrenees, right up to high altitudes, and may be seen on any fine evening throughout the warmer seasons, or on occasional warm days in winter. The species include representatives of the horseshoe bats, as well as the more frequent species such as

31. On the French side, there is a huge forest of beech and fir covering the western slopes in the Iraty area—the sole remaining Pyrenean site for the brown bear.

noctule, serotine, pipistrelle, etc. They are very difficult to identify to species level without expert knowledge or special equipment.

Red squirrels, *Sciurus vulgaris*, are common in forested areas throughout the Pyrenees. Although more commonly associated with coniferous forests, they also occur in Pyrenean beech and mixed forests. They are frequently active and visible during the day, and are often detected by their chattering call. The remains of pine and other cones, with the discarded scales spread around, are a good sign of their presence.

Alpine marmots, *Marmota marmota*, are beautiful rodents, related to squirrels but much larger. They are distinctive by virtue of their size (up to 75 cm, 30 inches, head to tail), their large bushy tail, and their piercing whistle call. They have been reintroduced to the central Pyrenees, and are now reasonably common in parts of the French National Park, in high rocky valleys above the tree line. They are active by day, but most seen in early morning or late afternoon and evening.

Pine martens, *Martes martes*, **Beech martens**, *M. foina*, and **polecat**, *Mustela putorius* all occur in the forested areas of the Pyrenees, though they tend to be nocturnal, so they are rarely seen by the casual observer.

Otters, *Lutra lutra*, are beautiful relatives of the weasels, highly adapted to aquatic life. Although quite common in the Pyrenees, they are solitary, shy, and mainly nocturnal, so you have to be lucky or diligent to see one.

The **genet**, *Genetta genetta*, is a little-known but highly distinctive animal, reminiscent of a racoon. Including their long tail, they may reach a metre or more in length, with a dark, spotted coat, and a marvellous dark-ringed bushy tail. They live in wooded areas, up to about 2000 m (6500 ft), and are mainly nocturnal predators.

The **lynx**, *Felis lynx*, is exceptionally rare in the Pyrenees, and there is some doubt over whether it still occurs at all. Its large size, tufted ears and spotted coat make identification relatively easy in the unlikely event of seeing one.

Wild boar, *Sus scrofa*, are common in the lower wooded areas of the Pyrenees, on both sides, though they are not a mountain animal and can be as common in adjacent lowland areas. Look out for areas of disturbed turf where they have been feeding.

Mouflon, *Ovis musimon*, are close relatives of the sheep that occur as a naturalized introduction in the central Pyrenees. They have the build of a domestic sheep, but their coats are hairy rather than woolly, reddish brown with a pale flank patch, and with robust curled horns.

Ibex, *Capra pyrenaica*, occur in their Spanish form, which has rather different horns compared to the Alpine counterparts, less ribbed and more outward-curving. They are surprisingly common in high rocky areas, mainly on the southern slopes.

Chamois, *Rupicapra rupicapra*, are much more common than ibex, occurring almost throughout the range. They are particularly common in Ordesa; one of us was once there on an evening in April, and, on getting up from a long session in a hollow photographing snowbells, found a herd of about 30 animals grazing all around the hollow! The coat is light brown in summer, and darker and shaggier in winter, and they have short curved horns on both males and females.

Several species of deer occur in the Pyrenees, including **red deer**, *Cervus elaphus*, **fallow deer**, *C. dama*, and **roe deer**, *Capreolus capreolus*, mainly in lower wooded areas.

BIRD LIFE

As with the mammals, the birds of the Pyrenees are a wonderful mixture of lowland species, formerly-widespread species finding refuge here, and mountain specialists. The range is further widened by the coming and going of summer and winter migrants, the altitudinal migrations of many species, and the spectacular movements of passage migrants going south in autumn and north again in spring. Again, we can only select a few specialities and species of interest from the hundreds of species which occur in the Pyrenean area.

Birdwatching in the Pyrenees

Almost anywhere in the Pyrenees is good for birds, though lower cultivated areas generally hold lower numbers and fewer mountain specialities. The National Parks are all good, and it is always worth checking around high-altitude cafés, ski-huts and car parks for tame mountain birds such as choughs, snowfinches, etc.

Carry a good pair of binoculars, and use them constantly to scan cliffs, the sky, trees, bushes, etc., and to help see diagnostic features of distant birds for identification.

It is often worth sitting for a while in a good area, with a pair of binoculars, and scanning the skies and the area around about. This will often produce more than when constantly on the move.

As with mammals, it is best to walk quietly and unobtrusively, constantly scanning the land ahead.

Black kite, *Milvus migrans*. A summer visitor to the Pyrenees, breeding throughout much of the area, it is probably the bird of prey most often seen in summer.

Red kite, *M. milvus*. A beautiful and distinctive bird of prey which is reasonably common and widespread in the Pyrenees, as a partly resident population boosted by summer migrants. The long, deeply-forked tail, reddish underparts, and white patch on the wings help to identify it. It mainly occurs around wooded areas.

The **lammergeier**, *Gypaetus barbatus*, is an incredible bird which has one of its main European headquarters in the southern Pyre-nees. It is huge with a distinctive outline of long narrow wings and wedge-shaped tail, and a 'beard' of feathers, giving it its alternative name of bearded vulture. It breeds in high rocky areas, and is not infrequently seen gliding along valley sides, looking for carrion.

The **griffon vulture**, *Gyps fulvus*, is a huge vulture, with a typical vulture shape of broad, straight wings and short, square tail. They are, at last, beginning to increase again in the Pyrenees after years of decline, and are now quite a familiar sight, especially in Spain and around Gavarnie and the Pic du Midi de Bigorre area in France. The **Egyptian vulture**, *Neophron percnopterus* is much smaller, mainly white, and much less common, coming as a summer visitor for breeding.

Various eagles occur in the Pyrenees, including the **golden eagle**, *Aquila chrysaetos*, **booted eagle**, *Hieraaetus pennatus*, **Bonelli's Eagle**, *H. fasciatus*, and the **short-toed eagle**, *Circaetus gallicus*, though you need a good bird book to distinguish one from another. There are also **buzzards** and **harriers**, amongst other birds of prey.

The **rock thrush**, *Monticola saxatilis*, is an attractive and distinctive bird that has become more common recently, and taken to nesting in and around the chalets of ski resorts. The males have a blue head, a red breast and a white rump, and they are common in rocky areas.

The **wallcreeper**, *Tichodroma muraria*, is a highly-specialized and distinctive mountain and cliff dweller. It has a long curved bill, short rounded wings, and a short tail, and is basically grey and black, with crimson patches on the wings. It is the only bird likely to be seen working its way up a rock face, often at considerable altitude, then flying down and starting at the bottom again.

There are two species of **chough** in the Pyre-nees—the **Alpine** (or **yellow-billed**) **chough** and the **chough** (or **red-billed chough**). Both are black birds, the size of jackdaws (to which they are related), but with red legs and colourful, curved beaks. As the names suggest, the Alpine has a yellow bill, while the 'common' chough has a red bill. Both occur in high pastures around cliffs, though the Alpine tends to be at higher levels, and is particularly in evidence around high settlements in winter. They are both delightfully aerobatic birds, with mellifluous calls.

The **raven**, *Corvus corax*, is another member of the crow family that is particularly found in mountains, though by no means confined to them. It is common in the higher parts of the Pyrenees, where its guttural croaking is a familiar sound. Ravens are much bigger and heavier than choughs, and are all black.

Snowfinches, *Montifringilla nivalis*, are true mountain species, frequenting the highest levels of the Pyrenees and staying well up in the mountains in winter. They have adapted well to the skiing life, frequenting ski villages in winter for food. In flight they look markedly black-and-white, often occurring in small resplendent flocks.

REPTILES AND AMPHIBIANS

There are relatively few special reptiles and amphibians in the Pyrenees. Any visitor will almost certainly notice the lizards, which occur throughout, and these are a complicated and difficult group to identify, as many common European species occur together in the Pyrenees, often in unusual colour forms.

One extraordinary animal is the **fire salamander**, *Salamandra salamandra*, which occurs in damp places, often in woods, up to about 2000 m (6500 ft). It is a strikingly-coloured creature, black with bright yellow-orange spots, but rarely seen because it is nocturnal in its habits. The **Pyrenean brook salamander**, *Euproctus asper*, is confined to the Pyrenees, but is a smaller and much less boldly-marked animal, brown with yellowish or cream spots and stripes. It occurs in and around cold mountain lakes and streams, especially at about 2000 m (6500 ft) up. Other amphibia include toads, spadefoots, tree-frogs, common frogs and a number of other species, whilst reptile species include various kinds of snake.

INVERTEBRATE LIFE

Even to the casual observer, the invertebrate life of the Pyrenees—that is, the insects and their relatives—is something special. The flowery meadows and pastures are alive with butterflies, grasshoppers, crickets and innumerable other insects; flying, mating, feeding and calling. Unfortunately, the number of species involved is just so vast, even if you reduce it to the mountain specialists only, that it is impossible to begin to do justice to them here. The best advice is to take along a good book—there are many specialist ones covering the well-known groups, such as butterflies, dragonflies, grasshoppers and the like, and several good general guides. Start by trying to work out the commonest and most distinctive species . . . or just enjoy the spectacle, without bothering over what species are involved!

A very few species are worth mentioning, though, because we know they are ones that people do notice particularly.

Amongst the many grasshoppers, there are several striking species that have a large band of colour on their wings, that 'flashes' as they take flight. Probably the commonest montane species is the red-flashing species, *Psophus stridulus*, but there are also species with blue or greenish flashes.

Field crickets, *Gryllus campestris*, are abundant throughout the Pyrenees, and they are most often heard rather than seen, as the male sits at the mouth of his burrow singing. If you catch them unawares, you see a striking shiny black insect, with yellowish band, and long antennae.

There is one insect that often attracts attention as it flies around flowery meadows and settles on flowers; they look like dragonflies, but do not behave like them, and their net-veined, broad wings, with large black spots, together with their long clubbed antennae, are distinctive; they have no common name, but they are related

32. Medium-altitude pastures spring back into life in autumn with a mass of late-flowering bulbs, such as these purple Merendera montana *flowers.*

to ant-lions, and are generally called ascalaphids, with the most frequent species being *Libelloides longicornis.*

There are so many butterflies that they would need a whole book to themselves, but one that stands out by its appearance and its high-altitude habitat, is the **Apollo**, *Parnassius apollo*. It flies lazily in the sunshine in high pastures and rocky areas, visiting flowers and displaying its white wings, with black and red spots. The caterpillars feed on stonecrops and houseleeks, which are abundant here.

One final insect that often strikes visitors to the Pyrenees—literally, on occasion—is the **stag beetle**, *Lucanus cervus*. The males are huge black beetles with large red (harmless) 'horns', and they emerge in early summer on warm evenings to fly noisily, slowly and almost uncontrollably through the air in search of females. Their larvae live in dead wood, taking many years to develop, and they have become rare in the managed lowlands. But the old forests and tree-fringed fields of the Pyrenees provide an ideal habitat.

CHAPTER SEVEN

Walking in the Pyrenees

France and Spain are countries of great variety, each with two coasts, various mountain ranges, a pleasant climate, superb food, excellent wines and friendly people—all good reasons for taking a walking holiday in the Pyrenees.

For the walker, both sides of the Pyrenees offer almost limitless possibilities for walks, ranging from rambles of a few hours duration to treks of several weeks. In terms of scenery and wildlife there are differences on both sides but, nevertheless, they are equally attractive to the walker. However, for ease of access along the whole length of the Pyrenean chain, France is especially well served by footpaths, some of which cross over into Spain. On the Spanish side, one can start with two National Parks (Ordessa and Mt Perdido; Aigüestortes and Lake Sant Maurici), where there are extensive marked paths to take you through incomparable mountain scenery.

THE GRANDE RANDONNÉE FOOTPATH NETWORK (THE GR SYSTEM)

A network of carefully-marked footpaths, some 40,000 km (25,000 miles) in extent, covers virtually every corner of France. Whether you want to walk in the Alps, explore the extinct volcanoes of the Auvergne, wander over the *causses*, or even negotiate the country around Paris, there will be a marked route set out by people who know the area well—local people with a love of walking in their own country and an incomparable knowledge of the things worth seeing. This network of paths is the creation of *La Fédération Française de Randonnée Pédestre, Comité National des Sentiers de Grande Randonnée* (FFRP), something of a mouthful but the result is the finest system of marked paths in Europe; the product of four decades of work. Some of the footpaths, marked with their familiar red and white bars, allow you to follow ancient pilgrim routes (Le Chemin de St Jacques—GR65) or to make mountain circuits (Tour de Mont Blanc).

As an added bonus, the footpaths are well supported by a wide range of comfortable country accommodation, offering a chance to sample local cooking and providing the opportunity to meet the people. Unlike Britain, where walkers are often treated with hostility by landowners, people elsewhere in Europe seem to accept walkers and invariably greet them: the people of the Pyrenees are no exception.

There are three broad 'classes' of route marking within the system:

Sentiers de Grandes Randonées—Waymarked by *red* and *white* dashes on rocks, trees, posts and walls, with additional marks to show the number of the path, direction and even a typical time needed for the walk.

GR de Pays—Generally circular tours, way-marked in *red* and *yellow*.

Petite Randonée (PR)—Local walks allowing rambles of a few hours or a day, usually marked along the way in *yellow*.

The FFRP produce detailed guides to the GR system of paths called *Topoguides*, and currently there are around 170 in print, compiled and written by local members of the organization—the same people responsible for marking the paths. Formerly available only in French, collections of these guides have been amalgamated and adapted to produce regional guides in English.

WALKS IN THE PYRENEES

France: GR10—*Sentier de Pryénées*

The GR10 route must rank as one of the great walks of France, with all the ingredients to make it a very special experience whether negotiated as a whole or taken in parts. Not only is there a tremendous variety of scenery, including coasts, farmlands, glacier-carved valleys, alpine flower meadows and snowfields, but there are also villages in incomparable settings. Although from coast to coast an energetic crow would cover some 400 km (250 miles), the GR10 from Hendaye to Banyuls is about 700 km (435 miles) and will take the ardent mountain walker five to seven weeks to complete—and that is a minimum because of all the diversions possible *en route*!

33. The extraordinary Breche du Roland, on the high ridge between France and Spain above Gavarnie, is a tough but attainable goal for walkers.

There is no compulsion to complete the whole walk, and parts make excellent outings within the framework of a touring holiday. If you want to dedicate a fortnight or more to the walk then it can be divided into convenient sections to give a wide experience of the different parts of the Pyrenees.

Spread along the route there are *refuges*, villages and *gîtes d' étape* offering accommodation, so it is possible to walk without the encumberance of a heavy backpack—unless you carry the weight of photographic equipment that both authors do!

The GR10 begins in Basque country beside the Atlantic at Hendaye and winds through lush valleys, wooded hills, gorse and bracken in a land kept moist by clouds and rain from the seacoast. The scene changes dramatically where the Basque lands give way to the High Pyrenees, and wooded country is replaced by limestone pavement around Pic d'Anie. The route passes through Lescun, which is a good place to stay to make detours into the limestone peaks forming the frontier with Spain. The Aspe valley, scoured by glaciers long ago, provides a dramatic vista before reaching the Pic du Midi d'Ossau, where a day or so can be devoted to the classic tour of this distinctive mountain. With more time to spend, there is the more demanding *Tour de la Haute Vallée d'Ossau*, which will take up to five days to do it justice. The GR10 avoids the difficult terrain of the Balaitous Massif and its forbidding granite landscape by passing to the north, but there is an official diversion which heads south to the Gaube valley to give stunning views of Vignemale, at 3298 m (10,280 ft) the highest frontier summit in the Pyrenees. Gavarnie is the next objective, to take in the spectacle of the Cirque de Gavarnie.

By winding in and out of the National Park, the GR10 eventually reaches the Néouville Massif, with innumerable small lakes and peaks inviting exploration. By descending to Bagnères de Luchon itself, the route copes with the anomaly that has made the Val d'Aran a part of Spain and forced the border northward (p 22). A contrast with the high peaks is provided by wooded hillsides and fast-flowing streams as it skirts Mont Valier (2838 m; 9311 ft).

Haut Arriège lies between Luchon and the Carlit Massif and the few roads make it wild, lonely country with deeply-cut valleys, which for the more adventurous can provide challenging walks away from the main GR10. The vista presented by the Carlit Massif, with its bare granite peaks and glistening tarns, is truly magnificent.

The heights of the eastern Pyrenees in High Catalonia can be extremely hot in the summer, but this is a new landscape of sunny hills and extensive orchards, with the Mediterranean beyond. It is difficult to think of anywhere else that can provide such variety as the Pyrenees, much of it accessible with only a little determination.

Anyone intending to cover all or even parts of the GR10 can find details of the route, with maps, in the *Footpaths of Europe* series (Robertson McCarta). The maps show the GR10 on the Institut Géographique National base maps, and so have all the detail needed, including a breakdown of average times for completion of each stage.

Spain—The National Parks

There are nine national parks in Spain and two of them lie within the Pyrenees. The National Park of Aigüestortes and Lake Sant Maurici in Catalonia was set up in 1955 and covers an area of 10,230 ha (38 sq miles), while the National Park of Ordesa and Monte Perdido in Huesca (Aragon) was reclassified and enlarged in 1982 to a total of 15,608 ha (58 sq miles). Both parks offer excellent opportunities for both easy and more strenuous walks on way-marked paths; and there are information centres where details and advice on route planning may be obtained.

The National Park of Aigüestortes and Lake Sant Maurici has superb granite peaks, cirques, U-shaped valleys, and is also a good place to see the Izard. To get to the Aigüestortes zone you take the N230 road from Lleida to Alfarràs, Benavarri and Vielha. After El Pont de Suert take the L500 to Caldes de Boi. An alternative route to El Pont de Suert follows the C147 from Balaguer to La Pobla de Segur and then the C144. The Lake Sant Maurici zone of the park is also reached on the C147 from Balaguer but before reaching Esterri d'Àneu take the LV5004 to Espot. In the summer months the tourist centres in Espot and Boi provide details of possible walks on the many tracks and paths within the park.

For visitors there are hotels in Barruera, Boi, Caldes Boi, Erill-la-Vall and Espot. Within the park there are four shelters providing basic accommodation and catering facilities: *Ernest Malfré* shelter (at the foot of Els Encatats, close to Lake Sant Maurici, accommodation for 36); *L'Estany Llong* shelter (located in the Sant Nicolau valley, accommodation for 57); *Amitges* shelter (close to Lake Amitges, accommodation for 80); *Joseph Maria Blanc* shelter (close to Estany Tort de Peguera in the valley of the River Peguera, accommodation for 30).

Further information concerning the park and the shelters can be obtained either from the park administration in Lleida (c/o Camp de Mart 35, 25004 Lleida; *tel* 973/24 66 50) or from the Tourist Office of the Patronat de la Vall de Boi Ajuntament de Barruera; *tel* 973/69 60 00.

Access to the National Park of Ordesa and Monte Perdido is gained via the 136 Cormacal Road from Huesca to Biescas and from there by the Biescas to Broto road through the mountain pass of Cotefablo. This takes you to the Ordesa valley while an alternative route to the valleys of Añisclo, Escuain and Pineta is on local roads coming from the 138 Cormacal Road from Ainsa to the French frontier beyond Bielsa.

There are numerous mountain shelters within the park but they only provide refuge from inclement weather and are not meant for overnight stays. However, there are several campsites and a Parador in the Val de Pineta.

A network of torrents eroded and moulded the limestone landscape over millions of years during the Tertiary period and it is in this dramatic scenery that the walker can start from an altitude of 750 m (2500 ft) and strive for the heights of Monte Perdido and other peaks rising to well over 3000 m (*c.* 10,000 ft). There are cascades along the River Arazas, canyons, cirques and a glacier to be viewed and photographed, to say nothing of a superb mountain flora and the chance to see golden eagles and lammergeiers wheeling majestically overhead as they soar on the air currents.

Whether the visitor is a hiker, mountaineer or rock climber, the park has a lot to offer. Starting from the car park at the bottom of the Ordessa valley (or from Torla) there is an old track which leads to La Cola de Caballo (the Horse's Tail) through a landscape of bizarre limestone formations and marvellous waterfalls. Another track from the same starting point follows the Cañon de Añisclo from San Urbez to el Barranco de la Pardina. There is a wide path from the village at Escuain which looks over the River Yaga as it flows through a series of deep gorges. A path leading from the Parador Nacional de Monte Perdido provides an easy climb to the Larri for views of the Circo de Pineta.

More demanding routes converging on the Goriz shelter either follow the hunting track of Faja de Pelay to the waterfall of the Cola de Caballo or proceed via the Cotatuero track. From the Goriz shelter one can then reach the heights of Monte Perdido, look over the Cirque de Gavarnie in France, cross the border via the Brèche de Roland or visit the frozen Grotto de Casteret—all in scenery of awe-inspiring magnificence.

High Route

The Pyrenees can be negotiated at altitude by a route that links many of the massifs and peaks. But whereas the sections linking massifs can be used by experienced walkers with the enthusiasm to do so, parts are very definitely in the realm of the climber and outside the scope of this chapter. For years, walkers of all kinds have used *Walks and Climbs in the Pyrenees* by Kevin Reynolds as a veritable 'bible' and we are no exception to this happy band of followers. It gives routes, times to complete stages, equipment needed and ways of gaining access by car to start walks. In the most recent edition, use is made of the High Route across the Pyrenees as a suggested means of linking areas for walking and climbing.

Maps

The French side of the frontier is served well by the publications of the IGN, which are accurate and coloured according to altitude in a way that makes them easy to read.

1:50,000—Recommended for the general picture they give with contours at 20-metre intervals.

1:25,000 (or 1:20,000)—These have 10-metre contours and are extremely well coloured, giving the reader a distinct 'feel' for the terrain. In addition, all IGN maps which cover the Pyrenees National Park have the main walking routes marked. There are separate maps with ski routes, so take care that you purchase the right ones.

Unfortunately, detailed maps of the Pyrenees south of the border are not of the same standards of detail and accuracy as the IGN maps. *Editorial Alpina* publish those recommended, which are either 1:40,000 or 1:25,000, contoured at 20-metre intervals and coloured according to altitude.

34. *View of the Ordesa valley from high on the slopes of Monte Perdido—a view that can only be seen after a long day's walk from the nearest road.*

In any moderately-sized Pyrenean town the shops will sell maps of the surrounding area but for those whose armchair planning is a part of the build-up to the holiday maps can be obtained in the United Kingdom through local booksellers (who can order if you know exactly what you want) or by visiting specialist dealers in London: Edward Stanford Ltd (map and guidebook stockist, 12–14 Long Acre, London WC2) and McCarta Ltd, (international map and guidebook distributor, 122 Kings Cross Road, London WC1X 9DS).

Organized walks

The tourist offices in any of the Pyrenean towns will have details of a programme of organized walks accompanied by local guides which are an excellent way of getting safely to some of the higher places. These can last a day, or can involve an overnight stay in a *refuge*. The cost is reasonable and it is a great way to meet people because of the camaraderie that links all those who love mountains despite the barrier posed by language. In a centre such as Luchon, for example, several such walks can be incorporated into a fortnight's stay, particularly on a family holiday where interests and demands might be diverse.

As well as individual, locally organized walks there are special walking tours and walking holidays. These are a very good introduction to the Pyrenees, even for the not-so-fit, since a few days of shorter walks in the mountain air can clear the lungs and put a determined spring back into anyone's step. Various Pyrenean treks, including special treks for birdwatchers and naturalists, are included in the programmes of a number of companies advertising in 'quality' newspapers, walking magazines and journals such as *Natural World* and *Birds*.

35. Walkers (far left) on a jeep-only track in the High Pyrenees by Lake Ratera, in the Aigues-Tortes National Park—a walkers' paradise.

GETTING THERE

Car owners or those prepared to run the expense of hiring a car will have no problems in getting to any starting point they choose for a walk. Sometimes it is possible to team up with a group of like-minded friends to provide good company, share the driving, and provide a means of cutting costs.

There are alternatives which are reliable, efficient and quicker than a car, particularly if one makes use of the excellent railway system within France. Indeed, two return fares compare very favourably with the cost for two people travelling by car when ferries, petrol and accommodation *en route* are included.

In the holiday season, there are direct flights from UK airports to Toulouse, Poitiers, Nantes, Perpignan and Montpellier, and in Spain to Madrid, which can get one well on the way, the remainder of the journey being completed via the SNCF (French railway system), RENFE (the Spanish narrow gauge lines) and country buses. In France, the only drawback to remember with buses is that they are usually limited to operate within a given *département* and getting from one provincial city to the next can pose problems unless there is a rail link.

When travelling by train it is necessary to go via Paris since all trains to stations serving the Pyrenees leave from the Gare d'Austerlitz, although straight-through tickets can be booked from any major UK station or travel agent with a British Rail agency.

As a guide, ways of getting access by rail and bus to different parts of the Pyrenees appear below:

Rail to Lourdes and SNCF buses: to Gedre for Barroude; Cauterets for Marcadau-Vignemale; Gavarnie for Gavarnie-Ordesa-Monte Perdido.

Rail to L'Hospitalet: for Carleit there is a choice of stations—Ax-les-Thermes; L'Hospitalet; Porté Puymorens and Porta.

By travelling instead to Perpignan you can take *Le petit train jaune*—the little yellow train—to Mont Louis.

From L'Hospitalet buses connect with the towns and villages of Andorra

Rail to Bagnères de Luchon (via Toulouse): for Maladetta.

Rail to Lannemezan on the Toulouse-Tarbes line: for Néouvielle by means of SNCF bus to Arreau and then by local bus to Fabian or St Lary.

Rail to Buzy: then SNCF bus to Laruns for Pic du Midi.

Rail to Lleida then RENFE train to La Pobla de Segur for National Park of Aigüestortes and Lake St Maurici.

WHERE TO STAY

Regular visits to France can spoil you because it is so easy to travel 'on spec' and find good food with clean, reasonably-priced hotel accommodation that you can become deluded into believing it must be the same elsewhere in Europe. Spain, in fact, has improved greatly over the years and small hotels are now almost as easily found there as they are in France.

It is possible to find good accommodation in the French and Spanish Pyrenees where the traveller will be welcome and the walker, in particular, can travel light. Throughout the Pyrenees, there are a number of different kinds of accommodation at prices that would prove attractive to the walker:

Logis de France are listed in a detailed guide published to this nationwide network of small, family-run hotels, offering comfortable accommodation and, as a rule, superb food. They offer excellent value for money and have a grading system from a basic one-star to the coveted five-star, where comfort and meals to satisfy the gourmet are a matter of course. The guide to over 5000 of these country hotels is updated annually and is available from the French Government Tourist Office, 178 Piccadilly, London W1V 0AI; *tel* (071) 491 7622.

Gîtes d' Étape (not to be confused with *Gîtes de France*—country cottages available for holiday letting) are virtually unmanned youth hostels for 'youths' of any age! They are to be found along the footpath networks and are specifically designed for walkers, climbers, cyclists, horse-riders and cross-country skiers: bunk beds, showers and a well-equipped kitchen are often the order of the day.

Youth Hostels are not nearly as widespread as in Britain and are often only to be found in main towns. A list of all those available can be obtained from: Youth Hostel Association (YHA), Trevelyan House, St Albans, Herts AL1 2DY.

Pensions and **cafés**—Enquiries at local cafés or bars will usually elicit information about rooms available for short stays. Often the café will have them or will certainly know of someone close-by who does.

Guest rooms (*Chambres d'hôte*) are the equivalent of Britain's bed and breakfast. These have become much more common in small villages and it is a chance to get to meet local people who will appreciate any effort you make with their language. As always in France and Spain, prices are per room.

Abris are mountain huts and shelters, usually run in France by *Club Alpin Français*. They are sometimes crowded and rather basic, not to say primitive. Some are available only to members and so it is worth joining the Club Alpin Francais, 7 Rue la Boétie, Paris 75008, France.

In Spain, as mentioned earlier (p 77), the National Park of Aigüestortes is well equipped with shelters that provide basic catering facilities, bunks with foam rubber mattresses and emergency transmitters.

Camping. Official French and Spanish campsites are invariably well organized, with facilities that can include shops, bars and heated pools in the best and be pretty basic at the other end of the scale.

Camping on farms is widely available in France and is a popular way of camping away from official sites. Pitching a tent just anywhere is not allowed in National Parks; but outside these, having the courtesy to ask permission will usually bring people to your aid.

Paradors

For those not familiar with them, the Paradors of Spain are worth getting to know about. They are a nationwide series of hotels, run by the government, but the special feature of them is that most are in restored ancient buildings of some sort.

These include monasteries, castles and forts. Although luxurious, the cost is reasonable for the facilities you get, and they can provide a welcome change after a period of camping!

In the Pyrenees, there are a few, though generally they are not of the highest architectural merit compared to some further south in Spain.

There are two new ones in the Val d'Aran, one in the Val de Pineta, and another in Andorra. They are usually signposted well in advance, sometimes at a distance of over 100 km (60 miles). They can be booked centrally, in advance, using the facilities of the national tourist offices.

However, the most interesting one in the area (and by far the cheapest), is a local version of the Parador at the monastery of San Juan de la Peña, southwest of Jaca (see p 99).

A small part of the ruined seventeenth-century upper monastery has been restored and converted to a bar, restaurant and hotel. However there are no signs to it, and you would not expect it on first seeing the ruined monastery.

It is in a beautiful quiet spot, and the pastures around are purple with *Merenderas* in autumn.

The Country Code—in France and Spain there is a Country Code which should be a matter of common sense for the responsible walker:

Love and show respect to Nature
Avoid making unnecessary noise
Destroy nothing
Do not leave litter
Do not pick flowers or plants
Do not disturb wildlife
Close gates after you
Protect and preserve the habitat
No smoking or fires in the forest
Respect and understand the country way of
   life and the country people
Think of others as you think of yourself

36. A modern Parador in the Val d'Aran—one of two large ones serving this area.

In general, walkers in France and Spain are free to wander on open paths and tracks without risk of aggression from irate landowners. However, it is always wise to be sensible and respect people and their country and, almost inevitably, you will be treated in the same way. Incidentally, chestnuts, mushrooms (of various sorts) or even edible snails are regarded as cash crops in some French districts and taking them might contravene local bye-laws!

WHAT TO WEAR

There is no need to load up like a packhorse if you are intent on covering parts of the GR10: you can find small hotels in the most unlikely villages. As a basic kit, there are items which should be essential depending on season:

Summer walking. Footwear is a matter of personal choice, though the advertising hype in magazines and journals would like you to feel you cannot walk another centimetre without their new, wind-tunnel-designed, ultra-hi-tech footwear. Both authors are inveterate users of strong training shoes (but make sure the soles are not the kind of plastic that slips on wet grass!). Lightweight walking boots and sturdy walking

37, 38. Two views of the ancient monastery at San Juan de la Peña, built partly into the conglomerate rock cliffs under which it is situated. Its position, high in the hills, is extraordinary.

shoes will fit the bill—in fact, use whatever you feel comfortable walking in and get a measure of protection from. For comfort, especially with those whose hair is becoming more 'economically distributed', a sun hat is an essential: shorts, suncream, sunglasses, lip salve and mosquito repellant can all prove useful. Pack a sweater—even in summer it can get cold towards the evenings—and a windproof and waterproof cagoule (road-test your old one before going on any walking holiday and re-

proof or replace if necessary). Finally, a small first-aid kit and a walking stick can help prevent discomfort later.

Winter walking. The chance of bad weather means carrying stormproof garments and a full change of clothing. If you intend walking high into the mountains an ice-axe and crampons are useful additions, summer or winter.

Whatever sort of pack you carry, detailed maps are essential (1:25,000) with a compass and perhaps a pocket dictionary, though above all, a preparedness to be patient with a ready smile will get one out of most potentially tricky situations.

Regarding health and emergencies, blisters are the most common problem for walkers, so it is important to carry plasters, but even more important to have footwear that is well broken in and loop-stitched socks to prevent blisters in the first place. Carry a water bottle and keep it filled in the summer, because the mountains are hot. In France, pharmacists will give first-aid treatment for a small fee (their shops are marked with a green cross). There is an obsession with snakes in some areas and you will see displays in pharmacists' windows advertising anti-venom serums and so on. There are two species of viper in France and Spain and most bites are caused by carelessness when an inattentive person just steps on the snake. If you see a snake, walk clear of it or stay at a few metres distance and let it move away.

There are cases of rabies (*la rage*) reported every year in France and Spain, as elsewhere in continental Europe. Rabies is a rare disease but the semi-wild dogs that one encounters in mountain villages should be avoided: any bite received should be treated by a doctor.

39. Waterfalls in the Circo de Soaso, Spanish Pyrenees, in an area that can only be seen and appreciated by walkers.

CHAPTER EIGHT

Climbing, Skiing and other Activities

THE EARLY CLIMBERS

The early history of climbing in the Pyrenees roughly parallels that of the Alps, though the Pyrenees have never become as popular and busy with climbers, and probably never will be. The number of distinct peaks is much lower, and perhaps the sense of achievement is less, though there is an immense range of possible climbs of all degrees of difficulty.

The Pic du Midi d'Ossau (2884 m; 9462 ft) is undoubtedly one of the most impressive peaks (or *pics*) of the Pyrenees, and it seems to have attracted the earliest attentions, being climbed first by a shepherd in the late eighteenth century.

The Vignemale (3298 m; 10,820 ft), on the high central border with Spain, and with a modest glacier on its north face—*Glaciere d'Ossoue*—has long attracted particular attention. The first recorded climb was in 1838, by a Miss Lister, accompanied by two local guides, but later it was made famous by the extraordinary Count Henry Russell. This eccentric gentleman was part Irish and part Gascon, and he took a particular fancy to the Vignemale, climbing it 30 times in all; eventually, in fact, he made it so much his own that he was granted a lease to it in 1889 (at a rent of one franc per year!). He was not merely a climber, but more of a mountain lover. His particular interest lay in constructing simple shelters amongst the high peaks, in which he would not only live, but also invite his friends to come and stay. The shelters were very basic, so his friends must have been a fairly hardy lot.

Gavarnie has long been a centre for climbers, and some who have died on the peaks are buried in its graveyards. The summit ridge above the great cirque proved a strong lure to early walkers and climbers, and there is a record at the Breche du Roland stating that it was reached by the Duchesse de Berry—carried in a sedan chair!

The Pic d'Aneto, in Spain, is the highest Pyrenean summit of all, at 3404 m (11,168 ft). Its ascent was attempted several times in the eighteenth century, and was eventually achieved in 1842, although it is not a particularly difficult mountain; the nearby Fourcanade is said to provide a much stiffer test.

CLIMBING TODAY

The climber visiting the Pyrenees today is presented with a marvellous array of climbs, from difficult walks or scrambles to the most difficult and demanding of climbs. More new and difficult routes are constantly being opened up, and the times for well-known routes are constantly being shortened. Not surprisingly, with so many large centres of population relatively close to the Pyrenees, French and—increasingly—Spanish climbers predominate, though the mountains also attract climbers from other parts of Europe, including Britain. Present areas

40. The cliffs of high cirques, such as this at the head of the Ordesa valley, are popular and demanding climbing sites.

of extension of new climbs centre on some of the huge rock walls, of tremendous height, that occur throughout the central region, and on the needle-like *aiguille* peaks, together with the re-climbing of summer routes under difficult winter conditions.

We cannot give details of specialized climbs in a book of this nature, and the reader is advised to refer to the excellent book by Kevin Reynolds on walking and climbing in the Pyrenees (see Bibliography), or to consult specialized climbing and mountaineering publications.

Accommodation and access in the Pyrenees are relatively easy for the climber. The general pattern of accommodation has been described in Chapter 7, and to this should be added the availability of high-level refuges which occur throughout the central Pyrenees. These are run by various organizations, but are open to the public, subject to space availability. They are not cheap, and it usually costs less if you are a member of the *Club Alpin Français* or the *Federacion Espanola de Montanismo*. In busy periods, i.e. high summer, it is advisable to arrive reasonably early to book yourself in; if you are with a group, an advance phone call (some refuges are on the phone) is advisable.

Accommodation is usually in communal bed-rooms, with huge shelves as multiple beds, often three storeys high. Large refuges can hold 150 people or more, but still get very crowded in season. Food is available, but varies widely in quality and quantity, and there is little likelihood of catering for special diets.

Despite their limitations, the refuges provide a wonderful way of seeing the high peaks, being in areas which are unspoilt, with, often, phenomenal views.

SKIING IN THE PYRENEES

We have a natural reluctance to talk about the Pyrenees as an area for skiing, since there is no

41. Skiing is promoting new high-altitude developments everywhere in the Pyrenees, especially in Spain, such as here at Candanchu below the Col du Somport.

doubt that skiing is currently the cause of the greatest changes taking place in the Pyrenees, and virtually all of them are detrimental. Development for skiing is proceeding apace in all three Pyrenean countries, and apart from the inherent ugliness of new ski villages, there are many side effects, such as the building of roads and tracks into previously unspoilt areas, a dramatic increase in erosion, disturbance of wildlife that is already under severe pressure through the winter, and an increase in pollution.

Nevertheless, it cannot be denied that the Pyrenees offer fine skiing, without much of the elitism associated with the best Alpine resorts. The scenery in winter is outstanding, and the weather is generally good. The season is relatively short, with February and March being the best periods. Facilities are constantly changing and improving, such that it makes sense to consult a travel agent specializing in skiing holidays, or to join an organization such as the skier's holiday guide club. A few companies specialize in ski holidays in the Pyrenees, such as Ski Miguel in Manchester. The following are some of the main ski resorts, by area:

Andorra

Andorra has several resorts, of which Soldeu/El Tarter, Pas de la Casa, Arinsal, and Arcalis are the main ones. Soldeu is the biggest. Noted for good weather and low prices, though the facilities and accommodation are rather limited. As in France and Spain, the extent of skiing is growing rapidly.

France

Ski resorts in France are extending rapidly within the Pyrenean area. The main ones include: Bareges and La Mongie (either side of the Col du Tourmalet), St Lary, Piau-Engaly, (at the head of the valley above St Lary), and Iraty. The weather is generally good, though the weather on the French side is more unpredictable.

Spain

Spain has come late to the skiing market, but their experience of tourism on the coast, and the amount of income that it generates, has led them to take to skiing in a big way recently. Extensive developments are taking place at present, especially in the high central areas, though the Spanish do seem to regard certain areas as sacrosanct. Major areas include the Col du Somport, and the Val d'Aran. The best known resort is probably Baqueira/Beret, in the beautiful Val d'Aran, which has numerous facilities and good accommodation, including two Paradors in the valley (see p ooo). Candanchu on the Col du Somport is a rapidly growing resort, and other areas include Super espot, and El Formigal (on the Col du Portalet road).

OTHER ACTIVITIES IN THE MOUNTAINS

The Pyrenees are developing increasingly as a leisure area, with consequent potential for various mountain-based activities. *Hang-gliding* is, not surprisingly, popular in mountain areas because of the distance you can travel, and the views you get. There is a school of hang-gliding below the Col du Tourmalet.

Canoeing and *white water river-rafting* are growing in popularity on Pyrenean rivers, and some areas actively encourage it in their brochures. Many rivers are best suited to these sports in winter and spring, when the levels are highest.

42 (following page). The cliffs of Monte Perdido, in Spain, are one of the most popular climbing areas, with numerous high-altitude climbs.

CHAPTER NINE

Driving and Cycling in the Pyrenees

By car

Having the use of a car for a Pyrenean holiday is a definite bonus unless one is content to choose a centre accessible by rail and make daily walks from there. Whether to take your own vehicle rather than to travel by air or rail and book a hire car in advance (or take a chance on hiring locally) is a vexed question of personal preference, time available and cost.

Both authors happen to love driving in France and the pleasures of travelling on comparatively clear highways and minor roads (especially between 12.30 and 16.00, when the attraction of lunch—a national institution—seems to clear the local populace off the roads!). Virtually every small town has an *auberge* where accommodation is priced for the room only (not per person) and memorable meals are to be had for the ordering. Thus, travelling south from a French port is not necessarily an ordeal: the alternative of taking the ferry from Plymouth to Santander in northern Spain involves a lengthy overnight crossing of the Bay of Biscay which can be uncomfortable even for those with good 'sea legs'. In terms of cost there is little to choose between taking a couple of days to travel through France with the fuel and accommodation thrown in and the ferry to Santander. If the object is to explore the Spanish side of the Pyrenees and wander further into Spain then the Plymouth to Santander ferry is well worth considering.

Out of season, it is easy to wander at will and find suitable accommodation on either side of the Pyrenees without the worry of approaching nightfall and nowhere to stay for the night. Accommodation can aso be booked in advance through numerous agencies and firms in Britain whether hotel, self-catering or even camping is required. If the idea is to stay away from main towns and resorts then national newspapers and magazines are an excellent source of privately-owned accommodation available for rental. Before choosing a locality, look carefully at a good map: although it is tempting to stay in a valley surrounded by high cliffs and mountains the variable weather in the summer can produce claustrophobic grey skies, and often there are considerable distances to travel and multiple hairpin bends to negotiate in order to get out of one valley into the next.

Staying higher up has its problems too—an altitude of 1500 m (5000 ft) can seem like the roof of the world as far as British mountains are concerned but in the Pyrenees it can mean being enveloped by a permanent soaking mist. At a lower altitude you could look up at these grey clouds only to see sunshine above them—but it is

43. Land-Rover trips can be arranged in some areas, such as here on the track to Ratera lake in Aigues-Tortes, to areas which cannot be reached by private car.

of little consolation when you are staying on the top of a col and the only way out is down! And ski resorts which look delightful with a blanket of pristine white snow can look far less attractive in the summer with eroded slopes and the debris of machinery associated with their winter use scattered around.

On the French side every small town or even village has its filling station but unleaded fuel is not nearly as widely available outside large towns as it is in the UK. On the Spanish side, it is just as well to start out with a full tank each day as 'insurance', since the temptation to wander on narrow roads can take one well away from civilization as the petroleum companies recognize it.

Cycling in the Pyrenees

Any visitor to the French Pyrenees cannot fail to be impressed and surprised by the number of French people cycling up the numerous hairpin bends of the cols with the intention of enjoying the exhilarating ride down the other side. Increasingly, people from all parts of Europe who holiday in the Pyrenees take cycles as part of their car or motorcaravan luggage, to use on arrival. The choice of routes is wide, with extensive land in valley bottoms providing possibilities for the less energetic, while for those who enjoy cycling up mountains the choice is endless. The advent of mountain bikes in recent years has opened up tremendous potential for those interested in covering forest trails.

Accommodation suitable for cyclists is detailed on p 83 and is basically that available to walkers.

Maps

An essential prerequisite for any holiday is a good set of maps and, for the motorist, general coverage of the French Pyrenees is well provided by sets of maps at scales of 1:200,000 and 1:100,000: Michelin 1:200,000 (nos 85 and 86); Institute Geographique National (IGN) 1:100,000 (nos 69, 70, 71 and 72).

For Spain: Michelin 1:400,000 (nos 42 and 43; Southern Pyrenees); Mapas Turisticos (Firestone-Hispania) 1:200,000.

ROUTES

The routes suggested are often 'circular', so they can be started or left at any point on the way. Never be afraid to take roads that look 'interesting'—that is part of the adventure with personal discovery of small villages, superb views, waterfalls and meadows adding to the magic. With common sense it is possible to travel virtually anywhere in the Pyrenees with a small car, however narrow the surfaced roads. Anyone intending to travel with four-wheel drive on forest roads would do well to ask the local Gendarmerie or tourist office about local restrictions and bye-laws.

Times and distances quoted are only a rough guide because we have found an irresistable temptation to wander. After the first few days of a holiday the winding-down process from the tension of normal living has well and truly begun and following a timetable becomes less and less important. Leaving plenty of time for detours and exploring small roads at whim is the only proviso we would heartily suggest.

1 The North Pyrenean Route—Bayonne to Perpignan
(Bayonne; Pau; Lourdes; Bagnères-de-Bigorre; St. Gaudens; Foix; Perpignan)
Duration—about 4 days : Distance—560 km (350 miles)

Stretching from coast to coast, this route represents by far the quickest way of negotiating the whole length of the Pyrenean chain. Not only does it provide excellent views of the distant mountains to the south but it takes in towns and cities rich in the complicated history of the region and allows diversions into the mountains proper at many points along its length. For anyone in a hurry it can easily be covered in a day's drive, but that would not allow for any realization of its potential.

Bayonne. The Basque name *Baï ona* means 'good river' and refers to the River Adour on which Bayonne stands. As well as being a Basque capital it serves the Landais to the north and Béarnais to the east. Its Roman name was *Lapurdum* and its prosperity depended on the navigability of the river.

Much of the fabric of the *Cathedral of Ste-Marie* has been restored after vandalism during the French Revolution. Twin spires were added in the nineteenth century. The knocker on the north door survives from the thirteenth century, when the building was started. At that time fugitives from the law could claim sanctuary as soon as they touched it—hence its name 'the ring of sanctuary'.

Léon Bonnat, a painter who died in 1922, had taught at the Ecole des Beaux-Arts in Paris where his pupils had included Toulouse-Lautrec, Munch, Braque and Dufy. He gave his entire art collection to his native town and the council built a gallery to accommodate it—the *Musée Bonnat* in rue Frédéric Bastiat. Many hours can also be happily spent in the *Musée Basque*, where the wealth of the exhibits illustrates the long history of the Basque people and activities as diverse as *pelota*, tuna fishing, whaling, chocolate-making, and local witchcraft are recorded together with the works of the early twentieth-century composer Maurice Ravel.

Pau, a city steeped in history, is the capital of the Pyrénées Atlantiques and from the *Boulevard des Pyrénées*, created by Napoleon III, there are outstanding views of the mountains. The *Château de Pau*, standing high above the Gave river, has lavish furnishings and a vast dining table capable of accommodating 100 guests. The castle is worth a visit for the tapestries alone, which include examples of Gobelins work and reproductions of earlier Flemish patterns.

Lourdes. Out of the high season for pilgrims (August and September), Lourdes has much to offer the visitor, with its great esplanade, three churches and a castle with an excellent museum of the Pyrenees. It is estimated that over three million pilgrims visit Lourdes annually (more than Rome or Mecca), many of them chronically ill, in the hope of another miracle. In 1858, it is claimed, the Blessed Virgin appeared 18 times to the young shepherdess Bernadette Soubirous and showed her the whereabouts of a healing spring—the one in the grotto from which pilgrims now drink. Out of the religious tradition has grown a local industry which offers gifts, souvenirs and curios of such astonishing vulgarity and tastelessness that it is hard to credit that anyone parts with money for them other than as a joke!

The spa town of **Bagnères-de-Bigorre** is a very good centre from which to explore the Pyrenees and also a popular holiday resort. The church of *St Vincent* dates from the twelfth century and there is a museum devoted to local interest—the *Salies Museum*. Close to the town lie the *Grottes de Médous* with fantastic well-lit stalagmites and stalactites, reached by boat.

Lying in the *département* of Haute Garonne and on the Garonne river itself, **St Gaudens** is another useful touring centre. Its twelfth-century church has a sculptured façade. Natural gas has been discovered in the district and there is a large local cellulose factory.

Foix can be reached directly from **St Girons** by following the N117. But for scenery and landscape views of distant mountains, the diversion via the D168 to Massat is worth taking. Foix is not really a tourist centre, but it has a remarkable triple-towered castle which dominates the provincial capital and is beautifully situated at the meeting of two rivers: the Arget and Ariège. In bygone days it enjoyed status as 'capital' for the Counts of Foix, in whose domain Catharism proved the most difficult to eliminate. Close to the town (*c.* 4 km; $2\frac{1}{2}$ miles) lies the underground river of *Labouiche*, reached by a road leading north from the castle to Vernajoul. There it is possible to travel by boat for over one kilometre (half a mile) through caverns with bizarre limestone formations.

A diversion on the N20 to **Tarascon-sur-Ariége** brings you to a town with a lovely riverside situation that could provide a base for further exploration. Just outside Tarascon there is a road which leads deep into the hills to **Vicdessos**: on it lies the *Grotte de Niaux* (see p 23), with its prehistoric wall paintings. By following the N20 through *Ax-les-Thermes* there is the choice of crossing the *Col de Puymorens* and travelling towards the Spanish enclave of *Llivia* (p 28) or negotiating the *Port d'Envalira* into Andorra.

Perpignan. The approach to Perpignan through urban sprawl can be offputting, yet the city's central part—the *vieille ville*—entered through *Le Castillet* (a fortified brick gateway of 1370) is delightful. There, the narrow streets with cobbled or marbled pavements resist the advance of 'progress' and it is fun just to wander. Near *Le Castillet* is the place de Loge with the *Loge de Mer*, built from huge blocks of dressed stone; its ground floor was once the *bourse*, or commercial exchange. The *Cathédrale-de-St-Jean* was started in 1324 by King Sancho, the second king of Majorca, and is famous for its altarpieces. Perpignan was made capital of the kings of Majorca and the small *Palais des Rois de Majorque* still stands, somewhat overshadowed by the massive walls of the citadel. The city has a number of museums: the *Rigaud Museum* devoted to paintings (including works by Tintoretto and Ingres); a *Natural History Museum* and others devoted to arts and crafts, and to coins.

2   The Western Pyrenees—The Basque Country

(St-Jean-de-Luz; Ciboure; Cambo-les-Bains; St Jean-Pied-de-Port; Pamplona)
Duration—2 days : Distance—210 km (130 miles)

St-Jean-de-Luz. The old port of St-Jean-de-Luz is full of narrow streets with their Basque balconied houses, some stone, some timber-framed, all bedecked with flower baskets and carrying a stone over the entrance which bears the date and a family name. In days before mineral oils, this was a whaling port and its wealth in the sixteenth century depended on a fleet of nearly 100 ships. At one time migrating whales appeared in the Bay of Biscay in spring and autumn but eventually, driven away, they were hunted further afield.

Across a bridge from the town lies the village of **Ciboure** where Maurice Ravel was born and where a community of 'untouchables' called Cagots once lived. Probably descended from lepers, they had no land and, shunned as far as marriage was concerned, both here and elsewhere in the Pyrenees, they survived as tradesmen.

The road to **Ascain** follows the River Nivelle. In summer, this pretty town with its typical Basque appearance draws trippers from the coastal resorts who are willing to spend a day away from the beach. **Espelette** is another typically Basque village on the route to **Cambo-les-Bains**, one of the numerous thermal stations in the Pyrenees (in this instance known for its sulphurous springs since Roman times).

From here a shorter trip is possible via **Ainhoa**, crossing the border into Spain at **Dancharia**. In this area witchcraft flourished from pagan times despite pressure from the Christian Church. Witches called *Sorgiñac* danced naked on the mountain summits on *akelare*—the Witches' Sabbat. The road climbs to the **Porte de Maya** then to **Elizondo** via the valley of Baztan—'rat's tail'. **Pamplona** is reached via the Puerto de Valete along river valleys and some dramatic rocky scenery.

St-Jean-Pied-de-Port. From Cambo-les-Bains the road follows the Nive to St-Jean-Pied-de-Port and the fertile country around it. The town developed to cater to pilgrim traffic, quite a lucrative trade in the Middle Ages, and still has a lovely old street within its ancient walls lined by Basque houses. In spite of the fact that the town has obviously geared itself for the tourist trade, it is useful as a centre for a more leisurely exploration of Basque villages off the beaten track. St-Jean, as the name 'pied-de-port' suggests, lies at the foot of the pass, and the road climbs up crossing the border to Valcarlos. **Roncevalles** (the Basques know it as *Ibañeta*) was part of the Roman *Imus Pyrenaeus* linking Gallia and Hispania. It is better known as the place where Roland, the paladin of Charlemagne's court, met his downfall (p 24). **Burguete** has become a place of refuge from the intense summer heat of the plains and a place from which to enjoy the fishing centre of the Irati valley, a wild, forested area away from the main tourist routes. From here the road leads down through the Basque villages of Zubiri, Urdañiz and Anchoriz, with a strange, eastern ring to their names, finally reaching **Pamplona**.

Famous for its bullfighting, particularly during the festival of San Fermin (p 45), Pamplona has other attractions for those who cannot be classed as *aficionados* of the national ritual. Those who might find a spectacle ending in the contrived death of an animal as nothing worthy of celebration, and a sad reflection on humanity, still have the cathedral, the *Basilica of San Ignacio* and the *Museo de Navarra* to take their attention.

3 Parc National des Pyrénées and High Aragon
(Pau; Oloron-St-Marie; Jaca; Gabas; Laruns)
Duration—2 days : Distance 217 km (135 miles)

By crossing the Pyrenees—in one direction by the *Col du Somport*; in the opposite direction via the more difficult *Col du Pourtalet*—there is a chance to travel through some stunning mountain scenery, enjoying the views.

Starting this circular tour from Pau, take the N134 to the twin towns of **Oloron–Ste-Maria**.

Until 1858 there were two communities on either side of the Gave d'Oloron, but nowadays they are administered as one. There are two cathedrals: *Cathedral of Ste-Maria* (completed in 1102) and Oloron's *Cathedral of Ste-Croix*. From the bridge over the *Gave d'Aspe* leading from one community to the other there is a fine view of all the peaks that surround the Vallée d'Aspe, including the Pic du Midi d'Ossau and Pic d'Anie providing a backdrop to the old town.

The road to the Col du Somport follows the River Aspe on one side and the old Canfranc railway on the other, through the fertile Val d'Aspe, until **Etsaut**, where the sides close in to form a deep gorge—*Port d'Enfer*—with a castle—*Fort du Pourtalet*—above. *Summus Portus* (contracted to 'Somport') was the only pass in the region until le Perthus (used by Hannibal) came into use. After the customs post in Urdos the road climbs slowly with jagged peaks for company—most well over 2400 m (7875 ft). On the Spanish side the descent is easier and takes one through the winter sports centre of Candanchu. At **Canfranc-Estacion** the old railway emerges from its tunnel and road and railway follow the waters from the head of the River Aragon down to Jaca.

Jaca. King Ramiro I of Aragon chose Jaca as his capital in 1033 and began the building of its cathedral. Now, it is one of only three towns of any size in the Spanish Pyrenees and plays host to a Centre for Pyrenean Studies run under the auspices of the University of Zaragoza.

To make the return journey take the C134 east of Jaca to **Sabiñáningo**, a small industrial town, then north following the Gallego River to **Biescas** and then **Escarilla**. The road becomes steeper and twists through the Garganta del Escaler and thence to the thermal resort at the **Baths of Panticosa**. After the tunnel beyond Escarilla the road passes **Sallent de Gallego** and climbs to wind around the southern flank of the *Pic du Midi d'Ossau* and over the *Col du Pourtalet*. For those who love wild places this is a

paradise, both scenically and for the animals that survive there—Pyrenean bear, wild boar, lizards and soaring eagles (p 69). The road descends through **Gabas**, another thermal station, and then **Laruns**, famous for cheese made from ewes' milk.

4 Ordesa

The road eastwards from **Biesca** leads to Broto and Torla and a chance to walk in the magnificent National Park of Ordesa, with its remarkable limestone landscapes. It is quite simply a paradise for anyone with an interest in the natural world and well worth exploring thoroughly on foot (p 77).

44. The impressive view greeting the motorist or cyclist emerging on the north side of the Tunel de Vielha, Spain.

5 Lourdes, Cauterets, Gavarnie
Duration—2 days : Distance—200 km (124 miles)

The charms, or otherwise, of Lourdes can be left behind by taking the road to **Cauterets** a winter sports centre and spa overlooked by the giant *Vignemale* (3298 m; 10,820 ft). From here there is a road to **Pont d'Espagne**, the starting point for numerous walks in the High Pyrenees. The road

45. A partially-ruined, isolated, medieval church in a village below Ordesa, Spain.

from Lourdes passes through **Argelès-Gazost** before it divides at **Soulom** with the choice of travelling to **Cauterets** or **Luz–St-Sauveur** (another amalgamation of two towns on opposite sides of a river, this time on the Gave).

From Luz a detour is possible via the *Col du Tourmalet* and round the southern slopes of the *Pic du Midi du Bigorre*, with its observatory visible on the summit, then back to **Bagnères-de-Bigorre** or via the *Col d'Aspin* to **Arreau**; from here the road leads south via the **Bielsa** tunnel into Spain.

Gavarnie and its famed *Cirque* (whose flowers are mentioned on p 61) lie beyond the village of **Gèdre**. The cirque is a stupendous 'amphith-eatre' formed by tall surrounding peaks of granite, and one of the waterfalls, the *Grande Cascade*, drops for over 400 m (1300 ft), making it Europe's highest. The *Cirque de Troumousse* is not as magnificent, but still worth viewing via the *Gave de Héas*. The area is an excellent centre for walking, enabling one to gain the heights with a little determination (see also p 61).

6 Bagnères-de-Bigorre and Lac de Cap de Long

Duration—2 days : Distance—180 km (110 miles)

The road over the Col d'Aspin has already been mentioned as a way into Spain via Arreau. The road from **Bagnères-de-Bigorre** takes the same route but to reach the lakes of *Orédon* and *Cap de Long* means turning right before the road reaches **Aragnouet** and travelling along the D929 for about 25 km (15 miles). Scenically, the journey is magnificent. The road to the Lac de Cap de Long climbs, with the Lac d'Oredon below, surrounded by woods and mountains. The terrain opens out as the high lake is approached and the jagged teeth of mountain peaks surround it. The stony terrain with its pine and juniper scrub, is good for wild flowers, and with a certain amount of scrambling one can get up high above the lake and enjoy a breathtaking panorama.

7 Luchon and Val d'Aran

Bagnères-de-Luchon is a true Pyrenean resort, offering winter sports, thermal baths, good shopping, plenty of hotels and opportunities for innumerable mountain walks of all degrees of difficulty. A rack and pinion railway leads up to **Superbagnères**, where the thermal springs originate, and the views are superb. Travelling down the valley to the village of **Cierp**, you take the turning to **St Béat** and follow the road to the border at **Melles**. This route is used by French locals who do their shopping on the Spanish side, in supermarkets close to the border where goods—particularly spirits—are noticeably cheaper. For some who try to beat the system and purchase more than they should, the sense of victory is short-lived even if they cross the border home, because they can be stopped by Gendarmes patrolling for the purpose! The road crosses the Garonne at the *Pont du Roi* and in high summer, the buddleia bushes, which seem to have colonized the river banks, are alive with innumerable butterflies.

The road runs along the **Val d'Aran**, which should really be a part of France (see p 22), where villages perch high up on the valley sides. Some of the houses have been very tastefully restored using local stone and wood, and are available on a self-catering basis for holidays in a region where the potential for walking is unlimited.

By turning east at Viella you can get to **Salardu** and over the *Puerto de la Bonaigua*, the country of the *Encantados* (the Enchanted Mountains)—an apt name for the jagged peaks. The road over the pass has been improved but, if you have a sense of adventure some of the 'roads' up the side-valleys are worth trying, slowly and carefully, if only because the views of the snows on *Maladetta* and luxuriant displays of wild flowers are well worth seeing. The track from **Salardù** to the **Pla de Beret** goes through **Bagerque** providing stunning views and a wide boggy area where the infant Noguera Pallarésa River meanders and the flowers of early summer vanish when thousands of horses are allowed to graze there.

The possibilities for the real wanderer are endless: travelling beyond Viella and through the tunnel allows a turning west towards Benasque and High Aragon on narrow, empty roads and, with a good map, to loop backwards and forwards in the southern Pyrenees, finding one's own secret places.

46. *The town of Bagnères de Luchon, in the French Pyrenees, is an ideal centre for touring by car or bicycle, with easy access to the high mountains.*

47. View from the main road up to the Puerta de la Bonaigua, in the Val d'Aran, Spain.

CHAPTER TEN

Pyrenean Architecture and Buildings

Mountains in general, including the Pyrenees, are not normally noted as places of particular architectural interest. For one thing, the people who lived in the mountains rarely had much spare money for major public buildings, nor were populations dense enough to warrant large religious buildings. Equally, because cities and large towns are absent or rare, there are no large concentrations of old and interesting structures, so the attentions of tourists with an interest in buildings are turned elsewhere.

Nevertheless, the Pyrenees have a remarkable amount to offer those interested in architecture, perhaps more so than most European mountains. Apart from the interest of nearby major towns such as Pamplona in Spain, or Lourdes in France, there is a considerable range of buildings of interest in the mountains themselves. This range includes both the grander edifices with religious and military origins, and many of the smaller towns and villages themselves. Pyrenean villages, on both sides of the range, are much more attractive than, for example, most French Alpine villages, and they are much less spoilt by modern (especially ski-related) developments.

Although there are both older and more recent buildings, the great majority of interesting ones are essentially medieval, spanning the Romanesque period—from about the tenth to twelfth centuries. There was an intensive period of Christian edifice building in the early part of this period, related to the retreat of Islamic influence and the development of Christian pilgrim routes to Santiago de Compostela. This small town in north-west Spain became a vitally important shrine in the early Middle Ages, and pilgrims came from all over Europe to visit it. Most of them had to cross the Pyrenees to get there, and particular routes developed, along which the current styles of architecture spread in the form of churches, shrines, hospices and other buildings.

Throughout the Pyrenees, walled citadel villages were built, mainly dating from the twelfth and thirteenth centuries. They were often purpose-built, and are therefore all of one style or age, though many have changed, deteriorated or been added to since. Villefranche de Conflent in the eastern French Pyrenees is a good surviving example, though there are a number of others. Many towns were walled later, especially by Vauban in the seventeenth century after the treaty of the Pyrenees.

The smaller, less significant or less wealthy villages often have a great style and character of their own. Their construction relates to the environment, to local materials available, to agricultural needs, and to particular local styles of building. Generally they are stone-constructed houses, with slate roofs, though styles vary. Basque farmhouses are often striking edifices, strongly built on a timber frame with a deep tiled roof, balconies and galleries. Many

date from the seventeenth century, and they are seen as symbols of the wealth of the family.

Agricultural buildings in the Pyrenees are also worth a second glance. They scatter up the hillsides beyond the highest villages as barns in the corners of fields, finally giving way to the huts used as living quarters in the summer pastures, known, amongst other names, as *olhas* or *estives*. The shapes of these barns and huts vary enormously, from triangular without walls to quite high-walled, solid structures; and they may have thatch, or wooden, slate or stone shingles as their roofing material. Some are very old, and many are falling into disrepair from lack of use.

The following gazetteer suggests some of the

48. Domestic architecture in a group of old cottages alongside the river in Arties, Val d'Aran.

more important, significant and attractive buildings of the Pyrenees, concentrating mainly on those that are well up in the mountains, rather than those of the surrounding lowland cultures. It is clearly by no means an exhaustive selection, and, as suggested above, there are attractive buildings at every turn in the lower and middle altitudes of the Pyrenees, even though they may not all be of historical significance. The lists are separated into countries, then treated alphabetically.

FRANCE

Cathar strongholds. The story of the eradication of the Cathars, or Albigensians, is one of the saddest and most brutal episodes in medieval history. For their beliefs, which threatened established Christianity, they were persecuted and killed, retreating to a number of spectacular castle strongholds, all of which eventually fell. Those at **Montsegur** (scene of the final tragedy), and **Peyrepertouse** are particularly spectacular and interesting, though they are in ruins. The main Cathar area lies east of Foix.

Luz-St-Sauveur is an attractive old town with numerous buildings of interest, and some good views of the central Pyrenees. The church of St

49. Castillon de Larboust, an attractive mainly medieval village near the Col de Peyresourde, French Pyrenees.

Andre is a fascinating thirteenth-century building, surrounded by a crenellated curtain wall with a beautifully carved Romanesque gateway.

St Bertrand de Comminges is a citadel town with an exceptional church/cathedral, part Romanesque and part Gothic, with other additions. It contains many features of interest.

50 *An old stone barn in flowery montane pasture, French Pyrenees near Luchon.*

51. *(right) The ancient gateway into the old part of St Jean Pied-de-Port.*

St Jean Pied-de-Port is an attractive medieval town set astride the River Nive. It is of great interest as a main staging post on the old pilgrimage route to Compostella, where several routes converged to cross the Pyrenees. There are many reminders of its pilgrimage past, including doors studded with brass cockle shells—the emblem of people going to and from Compostella. On one bank of the river lies the medieval town, crowned by a seventeenth-century citadel, whilst on the other bank lies a later suburb, walled around by Vauban after the 1659 treaty with Spain.

St Martin du Canigou is an impressive and beautiful old abbey, on the northern slopes of Mont Canigou, which dominates the Catalan

52. A wider view of St Jean Pied-de-Port, straddling the River Nive, with the old medieval town on the left, and the newer suburb—walled by Vaubin—on the right.

Pyrenees. The abbey has a spectacular position on the top of a rocky promontory high above the valley. It was founded in the tenth century, and is built in typical Catalan style, with a square tower, and a series of outbuildings around the tower. After a period of decline and dilapidation, it has now been restored as a religious retreat,

and guided tours are available to day-visitors. Not to be missed!

St Michel de Cuxa has an important abbey, which once dominated the area. It lies just south of Prades. The abbey was founded in AD 878, and added to later, and is unusual in France for being partly built in Mozarabic style (i.e. Spanish/ Christian, influenced by Moorish). It reached its peak of influence in the eleventh century, then declined into ruination, before being restored from 1952 onwards. It can be visited now, and there are guided tours and much of interest to see.

St Savin, just to the south of Argeles-Gazost, has an interesting example of an early fortified church in Romanesque style.

53. The striking seventeenth-century fortifications around the village of Villefranche de Conflent, floodlit in the evening.

Villefranche-de-Conflent is a strikingly attractive walled town in the valley of the Tet, south-west of Perpignan. It contains a mixture of buildings from the eleventh century onwards, including thirteenth-century round towers, and various seventeenth-century fortifications, including a fort, built by Vauban. It is best seen on foot, and there is a subterranean staircase linking the town with the fortress 160 m (525 ft) above it.

54. *The partly-ruined* Monasteria de Obarra, *on the Río Isábena, Spain.*

SPAIN

Bidassoa valley (Navarre). This is a distinctively Basque valley in the extreme western Pyrenees, containing the group of towns known as the Cinco Villas, where there are some fine Basque houses.

Camprodon (Gerona) is a picturesque mountain village, with a Romanesque church, and an attractive old bridge.

Jaca (Huesca) is a gateway to the Pyrenees, and a former stopping place on the pilgrimage route. Its cathedral is one of the oldest in Spain, dating from the eleventh century, in the Romanesque style that spread along the pilgrimage route.

Llivia (Gerona) is of interest as a boundary curiosity, since it exists as a Spanish enclave well within France. When 30 or so villages were ceded to France after the 1659 treaty, Llivia, because it classed itself as a town, remained Spanish. It retains an interesting fortified church and many medieval houses.

Pamplona (Navarre) is an attractive, small city, once the capital of the old Kingdom of

Navarre, and has always been the most important city at this end of the Pyrenees. Some historic buildings remain, including the mainly Gothic (fourteenth/fifteenth-century) cathedral, and an attractive old residential quarter.

Ripoll (Gerona). This is the site of an exceptionally important Benedictine monastery, founded in the ninth century AD by 'Wilfred the Shaggy'. It grew rapidly, and then suffered various changes and additions as a result of neglect, an earthquake and a fire. The present-

55. The cloisters of the extraordinary Romanesque cathedral at Roda de Isábena.

day mixture is an important and interesting site.

Roda de Isabena (Huesca) is only a small village, yet it has a delightful, perfectly-formed Romanesque cathedral, with ancient buildings around it, and fine views towards the Pyrenees.

Roncesvalles (Navarre) is famous from the epic *Song of Roland* (a highly imaginative

account of a defeat of the troops of Charlemagne by local Basques), and as a staging post on the main pass of the pilgrim route. Today, there is an Augustinian monastery, founded as a pilgrimage hostelry and chapel in the twelfth century.

San Juan de la Peña monastery (Huesca). An exceptionally interesting group of religious buildings, dating from the first foundation of a monastery here in the ninth century AD. The original monastery had another, Romanesque, church built above it in the eleventh century, and in the seventeenth century another monastery was built higher still (and later partially destroyed by the French). The construction, which uses the rock, is exceptional, and the situation is extraordinary, with marvellous views to the high

56. A general view of the Romanesque cathedral, which dominates the small, isolated village of Roda de Isábena.

57. The upper monastery at San Juan de la Peña, sacked by the French, is partly restored as a fascinating (and relatively cheap) place to stay. In autumn the pastures around are mauve with Merenderas.

Pyrenees. There are some interesting twelfth-century carving illustrations, depicting the history of man. Not to be missed, though its isolated situation involves a long journey.

Santa Cruz de la Seros (Huesca) was founded as a monastery in AD 992, though only the slightly later Romanesque church remains now.

Siresa (Huesca) is a tiny mountain village in the Valle de Hecho, with an attractive combination of houses and a fine church that derives from an original ninth-century monastery of San Pedro.

ANDORRA

The third country that has part of the Pyrenees

58. The mountain village of Santa Cruz de la Seros, near Jaca, with some attractive small houses, and the old Romanesque convent church (on the right), currently undergoing restoration.

within its borders, Andorra is a strange anomaly from a feudal age. It is a tiny country, with a map surface area of only 464 sq km (179 sq miles) (though rather larger on the ground, because of the steep relief and high mountains). Some aspects of old Andorra remain, despite the drastic pace of duty-free and ski-related developments in recent years.

In **Andorra la Vella**, the capital, there is a fine sixteenth-century government building known as the Casa de la Vall. In the mountain valleys

59. A small Romanesque chapel—San Caprasio—in Santa Cruz de la Seros, undergoing restoration.

running northwards towards the French frontier, there are a number of attractive villages with churches of interest, such as Canillo, St Joan de Caselles and Ordino.

Visiting Gardens in the Pyrenees

For most people on holiday, a visit to a garden or two in a new area is both interesting and relaxing, as well as stimulating. Unfortunately, though the Pyrenees can offer almost everything else, it is a poor area for gardens open to the public, and we have found very few of any substance. Basically, our advice would be *not* to visit the Pyrenees for gardens alone!

However, there are a few possibilities, though none are exceptional. The Monastery at St

Martin du Canigou has an attractive small garden in a beautiful setting. At Gavarnie, the National Park runs a garden that is more a patch of wild ground with additional wild flowers, and it needs a bit of looking for! Near Gabas, on the French side of the Col du Pourtalet, there is a National Park information centre, which has a well-maintained garden by it that contains many examples of Pyrenean plants, all accurately labelled (which is a great help). Finally, there is an arboretum at Joueu, between Luchon and the Hospice de France, run by a department of the University of Toulouse.

If you are travelling further afield, there are excellent gardens in Toulouse, Albi, Barcelona, and the Spanish coast near Gerona, at Marimurtra, Pinya de Rosa, and Cap Roig.

CHAPTER ELEVEN

The Photographer in the Pyrenees

The possibilities for photography in the Pyrenees are endless, and it is relatively easy to take good pictures there. Somehow, the variety of potential subjects, from snow-covered peaks and high valleys, through to masses of flowers, to close-ups of people at village markets or fetes, encourages people to take pictures they would not normally attempt or, perhaps, even be interested in.

Nevertheless, a huge amount of film is wasted by people who have the wrong equipment or film, or who have not prepared themselves; and an even larger amount of potential pictures go untaken by those who have either not brought the camera equipment to cope with them, or have run out of film, or who have not developed the skill of seeing good pictures. It is also true that a lot of potentially good pictures fail to materialize, due to camera faults, overheated films, X-ray machines, accidentally-opened cameras, and many other reasons. So, if you want to return with plenty of good pictures, go prepared.

ADVANCE PREPARATIONS

A large part of the secret of good travel photography lies in advance preparation, and while the Pyrenees are not a particularly remote or difficult area, they do pose certain problems that are worth planning for.

Selection of equipment

You may or may not already have all the gear you need. If you can buy things especially for the trip, you can choose carefully with the particular problems in mind. If you already have all the equipment you need, it then depends on whether you are travelling mainly by car, or intending to walk or cycle far, whether or not you take everything. If you are intending mainly to travel under your own power, then careful weeding out of inessential items is mandatory. In any event, try to consider, in advance:

1 the main types of pictures you expect to want to take
2 how much equipment you can carry, bearing in mind any other things you will have to carry, if you expect to walk or cycle far
3 the reliability and quality of your equipment
4 the use to which you intend to put your pictures

Looking at these in more detail: it is well worth considering carefully what you are likely to want to photograph. There is nothing more frustrating, for example, than to go with the intention of photographing wildlife, only to find that your lenses are not up to the job; conversely, it is pointless carrying around large heavy lenses if you really do not have a particular interest in using them. There is a problem, of course, in that you are never exactly sure what you will find (unless you are a regular visitor), so you tend to want to prepare for everything. However, your own interests, plus guidance from this book and other books, should help to give a reasonable indication of your needs. Several suggested 'outfits' are given later, to cover most eventualities.

If you are backpacking, you will inevitably have a considerable weight of other things to carry in addition to your camera equipment, so *weight and bulk become of paramount importance*. The weight can mount up considerably, and we suggest you try out your selected equipment on a full day-trip whilst carrying an appropriately-filled rucksack—you will probably decide to reduce the weight of something afterwards, but this is better than being unable to carry everything when you get there, or having a consistently miserable time from aching back and leg joints.

The reliability and quality of your equipment is important. Any mountain area, even the relatively civilized Pyrenees, is subject to high and low temperatures and extremes of weather, and these factors, together with perhaps weeks of bumping about in a rucksack, tend to expose faults in equipment that you did not know were there. The problem is compounded by the fact that you particularly want the pictures, yet you cannot see the results until after the trip, and you cannot usually do anything about any faults when they do arise.

Clearly not everyone can afford to buy the best-quality professional style equipment, which is the ideal; reliability and ruggedness undoubtedly costs money, though if your pictures are very important to you, then it is definitely worth considering a professional camera from Nikon, Canon, Minolta or Pentax. If you are managing with more ordinary equipment, it is wise to get it checked over and serviced well before you go, and have any faults corrected. After the service, allow yourself time to run a film or two through, to make sure the meter and other parts are correctly adjusted.

If you have neither the time nor the money to have your equipment serviced, then at least make sure you run one or two films through, then carefully check them for faults or inaccurate exposure. It is also worth remembering that main centres like Luchon have processing facilities for most films, and you can run a cheap film through the camera and get it rapidly processed just to test it; if returning to such a town in the middle of a trip, it can be very reassuring to check things over, or, alternatively, to discover and rectify any faults.

Finally, *the use to which you intend to put your pictures* is very important. If you intend to take 'snaps' to put in an album to show friends, then it is pointless spending a lot of money, and adding extra weight, in buying high quality equipment. By contrast, if you intend to write and illustrate a book of your experiences, or—often even more demanding—write and illustrate an article for a travel magazine, then you need to be sure that your pictures are of high quality, varied in content, and taken on good film. This will influence you to take a wider range of lenses, reliable equipment, and probably a range of accessories, including a tripod.

Suggested Outfits for Different Purposes

Minimum: A good quality, small compact camera, with or without auto-focusing. A small flashgun, matched to the camera if possible. 4–5 medium-speed films, in rolls of 36.

Average: A good Single-Lens Reflex (SLR), with automatic metering (e.g. Pentax ME Super), or an autofocus SLR (e.g. Minolta 7000) with 35–70 mm zoom (or something similar) as standard lens plus a 70–210 mm zoom lens for people, more distant views, some wildlife, etc. Polarizing filter. Flashgun. At least 10 rolls of 36-exposure film.

Advanced: 2 SLR bodies, preferably good-quality reliable ones. Autofocus or manual. Lenses of 28 mm, 35–70 mm, 70–210 mm zoom, possibly with 300 mm lens too. Extension tubes for close work; filters to include polarizing and UV. Tripod. At least 15 films (36 exp.), of more than one film speed, e.g. a mixture of 50 ISO and 100 ISO; or some Kodachrome 64, some Kodachrome 200. One body can be kept for views, etc. and the other, with faster film, for more difficult shots of people, wildlife, etc.

Cameras

If you just want to carry the very minimum, and are only interested in pictures of views, groups of people, rural activities, etc., then a compact camera, using 35 mm film, will be ideal. If you expect to pay about £120 (new price), you should get a good camera, with a high-quality lens.

If you are more serious about taking a range of pictures, to include, for example, close-ups of local people, flowers, wildlife, magnified shots of different peaks, etc., then you need a single-lens reflex (SLR). These all have the option of interchangeable lenses, so that you can take more than one lens and change it as required. Automatic focusing is quite useful, especially if you want to take lots of pictures of local people, e.g. shepherds, or market traders, giving you quick unobtrusive accurate focusing.

Lenses

If you buy an SLR, the range of lenses open to you is enormous.

60. *The domestic animals of the Pyrenees are well cared for and usually very photogenic, especially in low morning or evening sun. Cows on the col above Larrau, evening.*

A *wide angle* lens (between 24 mm and 35 mm, for preference) is useful for making the foreground dominate the scene, or for giving a great deal in focus. They are *not* especially useful for panoramic views, since they render all the background details smaller than you hoped, turning mountains into molehills.

Zoom lenses cover a wide range of focal lengths. Modern ones stretch from wide-angle, through standard, well into telephoto. For example, a number of 28–210 mm zooms are available. These are temptingly useful, as they cover all the focal lengths you may need in one lens. Their drawback is that they are quite bulky, so even for wide-angle shots or views, you still have to carry quite a sizeable lens on the camera,

61. Closer views of details can make interesting pictures, such as this neglected horse-drawn millstone at Roda de Isábena.

risking more chance of blurring through camera shake. Personally, we find 35–70 zooms to be excellent as standard lenses, with a good 70–210 mm zoom to cover the telephoto requirements.

Telephoto lenses are useful for wildlife, more unobtrusive shots of people, pulling in distant mountains or giving enlargements of mountain tops, together with interesting 'cameo' pictures, selected from a wider scene. A 70–210 zoom or a 200 mm lens will cover most general telephoto requirements; a 300 mm lens is more specialized, if you have a special interest in birds, wildlife, or other unapproachable subjects. Anything longer than 300 mm is rather bulky for carrying around, unless you are sure you need it. A *teleconverter* is a useful accessory, either as 1.4x or 2x magnification, to increase the focal length of whatever lens you have on. For example, a 200 mm lens plus 1.4x converter gives a 280 mm lens. They are light and small to carry. Make sure you get a good one (7 element, not 4 element, multi-coated).

To take close-ups, you can either take a specialist *macro* lens, or take one or two extension tubes, which fit behind the lens to allow any of your lenses to go closer. Close-up lenses, which screw on the front of lenses are useful, but liable to get dirty or broken, and you may need different ones for different lenses.

Some *filters* are useful in the Pyrenees, and in mountain areas in general. Ultra-violet or sky-light (which is slightly warmer) are useful all-purpose protective filters, and they have a slight effect of reducing the blue cast at higher altitudes, though it is not marked. If you keep them on the lens as protection, they do need to be kept very clean, to prevent flare or poorer quality pictures resulting.

The *polarizing filter* is probably the single most useful filter to take; it cuts out polarized light when correctly aligned, though this hardly describes its usefulness. Polarizing filters come in rotating mounts, and you rotate them to find the best effect, viewing this through the viewfinder with an SLR. They are especially useful for enhancing the blue of skies, cutting through haze, reducing glare, and preventing reflections from water. They can really enhance the colours of a picture and improve the colour of sky or the definition of clouds, though they are not always a good thing. (For example, they may get rid of reflections that were part of your intended picture, or make water look very dark.)

If you use black and white film, an orange filter will be the most useful single filter for most people. Square filters, such as the Cokin system, offer more choice and flexibility, but they are bulkier to carry and slower to use than conventional systems, so they are best avoided unless you are used to them.

Flashguns

An electronic flash is a very useful accessory in a number of situations, such as interiors, active situations in low light, night photography, small moving subjects such as insects, or, for the more experienced, as a fill-in light in natural light photography. The best option is a medium-sized (and medium-powered) unit, dedicated to your camera, and able to make use of the TTL flash metering if the camera has it. It helps to have a lead to use the flash off the camera at times, and this should transmit the TTL metering information if relevant. Spare batteries should be carried if you expect to use the flash much.

Tripods

If you are taking the production of photographs seriously, then taking a tripod becomes quite important. It allows you to get consistently sharper, better-composed pictures, with greater depth of field—for example, your landscapes could have everything in sharp focus from 1–2 metres in front of you, right through to infinity. The negative aspects are that you have to carry the tripod with you almost everywhere, and that it takes longer to take pictures, but the results are usually well worth it and will greatly increase the chances of having pictures published.

Film

Selection of film is a much more personal matter than cameras and lenses, though there are a few useful points to consider.

Film type can be slide (transparency), colour print, or black-and-white. In general, most people use colour print film, but the proportion using slide film tends to go up in areas like the Pyrenees, where more serious photography is done. If you only wish to produce an album or display to show friends, then print film is ideal. If, however, you are likely to give talks or lectures, produce an audio-visual display, or have anything published, then slide film is better; you can also have prints made from any particular slide, if desired. Black-and-white is a more specialized medium, and few people would take just black-and-white. Some books and magazines only want b/w, so you may find it worth taking some if you have this aspect in mind.

Film speed is a measure of how sensitive the film is to light. Faster films react more, and therefore allow you to use faster shutter speeds or smaller apertures in a given situation. However, they usually cost more, and are of lower quality, than slower films. If you only have one camera, it is best to take films of around 64–100 ISO, perhaps with one or two faster films for special circumstances. If you have two bodies, you can affort to load one with the slowest film you feel happy with, from ISO 25 to 64 (we usually take Kodachrome 25), and load the other camera with a faster film, from 50–200 ISO. Our preference is for a mixture of Kodachrome 25, 64 and 200, though other people prefer Fujichrome or Ektachrome. It is wise not to be tempted into a cheap offer of masses of film that you do not know, or which is out-of-date. Try anything first to make sure you like it. If using print film, there are numerous good print films of around 100–200 ISO, though again you should test it first.

Miscellaneous

Make sure you take spare batteries for your camera, if it works on them—there is nothing more aggravating than having your camera become inoperative miles from anywhere. Spare flash batteries are useful, too, and it is best to start out with fresh ones.

Cleaning cloths or tissues, such as those made by Prophot, are essential to keep equipment clean. A notebook and pencil as an *aide-memoire* completes the equipment.

EN ROUTE

If flying to the Pyrenees (e.g. to Lourdes), you will be faced with the dreaded X-ray machines at all airports. These pose a potential problem to photographers in that X-rays *can* fog film under certain circumstances. X-ray machines vary greatly in their ability to affect films, and films themselves vary in their sensitivity—the faster the film, the more liable it is to be fogged. As a general rule, take film with you as hand luggage, and, where possible, ask for it to be hand-searched rather than X-rayed, though this is certainly not always easy to arrange. If you have any fast films, pay particular attention to them.

If driving there, you have to bear in mind that film deteriorates very quickly in high temperatures, so it is worth keeping your films as cool as possible, preferably in an insulated box. Keep all camera equipment out of the sun as far as possible, and hidden from view.

IN THE HILLS

If you are simply motoring around the Pyrenees, you have few additional problems compared to photography at home, except that you use up film rather fast! However, if you are planning to walk much, either using the car as a base, or trekking and carrying all your gear, then your problems are much greater.

How you carry the camera equipment is important. If you have just a simple camera with no accessories, there is no real difficulty, except for organizing your exposed and unexposed films. If you have more equipment, though, you need some means of storing it with easy access. A waist-mounted Camera Care Systems bag (the 'Alternative workbench') allows rapid access to equipment and film, even if you are wearing a rucksack as well. Any large or less regularly-used items can be stored in the rucksack, along with exposed films and the main supply of unexposed film. Obviously, what you choose will depend on

62. *Wall with spring, covered with cobweb houseleeks—a typical Pyrenean 'cameo' picture, of the type to be seen almost everywhere.*

the amount of equipment you have, what else you have to carry, and what you are doing. Shoulder bags can be fine for a few days, but soon give rise to aching shoulders and even knee problems, due to walking unevenly.

If you are taking notes about pictures as you go along, in order to identify villages, mountains, or things people have told you along the way, then you need some means of identifying the films later. It is useful to have a spirit-based fine-point pen to write on each film as it is completed, or daily in advance if you only take a film or less each day. This can be cross-referenced to the notebook, and transferred to the film return address label when you get home. Keep both exposed and unexposed film as cool as possible, in a safe place.

Periodically, you should check the camera over. Examine the shutter, aperture, wind-on, etc., without a film in (but not on a windy day or anywhere dusty). You should also check the film chamber for any dust and carefully clean it out—dust can get into this section so easily, and it may scratch any number of films without your knowing. If you have two cameras, or a friend with a camera, it is worth periodically comparing meter readings to see that they are remaining accurate, followed by a shutter speed test. *If you change the film speed on one to make them comparable, remember to change it back!*

Opportunities

It is hardly necessary to take space to suggest opportunities for pictures—the problem usually lies in resisting them, rather than finding enough to take. A few suggestions may be helpful, though.

For landscapes and general scenes, it is well worth trying to get up early to get pictures with

63. Cattle grazing and resting in the Aigues-Tortes National Park—careful composition brings several elements together, and the framing branch (upper right) has also reduced flare by keeping the sun out of the picture.

greater impact. Dawn over the mountains from a good viewpoint can be very spectacular, and it is worth taking several pictures as the light changes. If you are near a lake, the early morning mist and soft light are likely to enhance the pictures. You will also often find that there are fewer people about and there is little wind, so it is generally a good time to be out. Evenings can produce some similar opportunities, and sunsets can be spectacular, though generally dawn is better.

Pyrenean flowers are really spectacular in places, and most people will be tempted to try photographing them at some time. Views including flowers look best on bright days, preferably with a few clouds around in the sky; close-ups of a few flowers or a portrait of one look best on hazy sunny days, or even in dull weather. The use of a tripod will allow you to set a small aperture, for maximum depth of field, though this may mean a long wait for the wind to drop and the flowers to stop moving.

Some Pyrenean people are photogenic, especially shepherds and market traders. It's worth visiting villages on market days, when there is always an interesting assembly of people and animals and some unusual things set out on the pavement in the sun.

Wherever you are, it is always worth looking out for close-up or cameo pictures that will enliven any talk or album. The detail on a stone wall, an old farm implement, the door of an ancient barn, or a cobweb covered in dew, etc., will all make interesting pictures. If you have in mind a particular talk or show that you propose to give, it is worth jotting down the range of pictures you want and making sure you remember to take them. It is very easy, for example, to forget to take pictures of your companions, of your house, or other everyday things.

Go well prepared and you are almost certain to come back with some interesting pictures to make anyone else green with envy!

Some technical points

There are a few points to bear in mind when taking photographs in the mountains, though generally the technical problems are the same as those elsewhere.

Getting the exposure right is straightforward in lower-lying areas, where there is the normal balance of light and dark tones, but the light meters of virtually all cameras will be confused by snowy conditions or large expanses of very light rock. All meters are calibrated to deal with average subjects and if faced with too large a proportion of a light or dark tone, they try to push it towards the average; in the case of snow or light rock, the meter will tend to expose these as grey, or darker than they are, i.e. it will underexpose. Thus, when photographing in snowy conditions, you need to overexpose by about one stop compared to what your camera's internal meter tells you. If you are photographing people, animals or other relatively dark subjects on an expanse of snow, you may have to overexpose by even more to get them correctly exposed.

At high altitudes in sunny weather, there is a very high proportion of blue in the light, and this will show up disproportionately on photographs. It is sensible to use a skylight filter, or a slightly stronger filter (e.g. Nikon's amber filter), to counteract this at higher altitudes. A polarizing filter, as mentioned above, is especially useful for cutting through haze, showing up clouds, and generally sharpening outlines by reducing reflections and scattered light. If using black-and-white film, a yellow or orange filter is invaluable.

CHAPTER TWELVE

Protecting the Pyrenean Environment

The first-time visitor to the Pyrenees will almost certainly be impressed by their unspoilt nature: the fields full of flowers, the absence of ugly developments, the extensive forests, and the lack of intensive agriculture. All these features *are* impressive, and the Pyrenees are one of the least spoiled of West European mountain ranges. Nevertheless, changes are taking place, and those who have known the Pyrenees over a period of years will have seen them. The obvious signs include greatly increased visitor numbers, new ski developments (both residential and associated lifting gear), new roads, meadows that become steadily less flowery, the replacement of natural forests by monotonous plantations, and so on. Less obvious are the steady declines in mammal and bird numbers that have taken place, in response to subtle changes in the environment.

Compared to the lowlands, and indeed to most mountain areas, these changes are relatively slow and subtle. The isolation of the Pyrenees, and their steep slopes, has made 'progress' slower, and much remains as it has been for centuries. The problem is that many of the changes that do take place are irreversible, or, at least, very difficult to reverse. While most people would accept that some change is inevitable, many of the worst changes are unnecessary or avoidable, and are often done simply to make additional money for international companies run by accountants, with few benefits to the local people. Unfortunately, the more subtle changes are, the more slowly we wake up to them and react to prevent them happening, until it is often too late. Strong, moneyed interests will also often act against the wishes and the benefit of the majority, maintaining their status by strong political lobbying. For example, few people could possibly wish to see the devastating and wholesale slaughter of migrating birds on Pyrenean passes continue, yet it does, unabated. In fact, the only factor that is reducing this unbelievable business is the fact that there are fewer and fewer birds to shoot. It is hardly surprising that if you shoot as many as possible of the falcons, hawks, doves, buzzards, songbirds, storks, and all other birds that have to migrate from northern Europe through the Pyrenean passes, without any regard to their age, sex or condition, then you will reduce the populations of these birds throughout their range, and correspondingly fewer will migrate back in successive years.

National Parks and reserves

The primary way of protecting landscapes, traditional ways of life and nature is through the creation of National Parks. Unfortunately, neither France nor Spain can be said to be in the forefront of international conservation— though Spain has a long history of protective legislation—and the protection is often neither strong enough nor extensive enough.

64, 65. Deserted villages are a common sight in the Pyrenees, especially on the Spanish side, such as these along the Rio Gallego. Sometimes they have been abandoned for reservoir construction, but other abandoned villages simply represent a dwindling rural population.

The French scheme involves a two-tier system in which there is an outer, or peripheral, park zone, managed locally with the aim of maintaining the local way of life (and often with local commercial interests in mind); and an inner core zone, more rigorously protected and controlled by a team of professional staff. The French National Park in the Pyrenees covers just under 500 sq km (193 sq miles) of the high central area, centred on Gavarnie and Pic du Midi d'Ossau. Although this may contain much of the most impressive scenery, it is also the easiest area to protect, with fewest conflicts, and it leaves a vast area of the mountains unprotected. Management is not strongly geared towards protecting the wildlife and flowers, and overgrazing, for example, is severe, even within the national park. Outside the park, the survival of traditional landscapes and natural life depends largely on a combination of chance and the harsh environment.

In Spain, there are two Pyrenean National Parks, Ordesa and Aiguestortes y Llac de Sant Maurici, which between them cover a little under 400 sq km (154 sq miles). Again, they protect the highest and wildest areas, though in this case the current management seems to work well and both areas are alive with natural life. Ordesa is one of the oldest of Spain's National Parks, dating from 1918.

In addition to the key National Parks, there are nature reserves, regional parks and so on, but collectively they cover and protect very little land, and often the designation is of little relevance in terms of protection and legislation. Unfortunately, mountain ranges, while seeming so robust and resilient, are actually very fragile ecosystems, and without care, forethought and management, their interest to the naturalist, historian, archaeologist or seeker after beautiful landscapes will quietly decline.

Vultures and livestock

To illustrate some of the subtler changes that are going on in the Pyrenees, and to emphasize the difficulties of protecting a mountain chain ecosystem just by preserving a few selected parts, it is worth looking at the story of the griffon vulture. Griffon vultures have always occurred in the Pyrenees, as they do in a number of other parts of Spain, nesting and roosting in high rocky areas and feeding on carrion. They developed a relationship with agricultural man, probably from earliest times, since the most abundant and accessible carrion has long been that of domestic animals' corpses. Until relatively recently, farmers appreciated the role of vultures in their economy, as automatic removers of sources of disease. The vultures would not attack healthy domestic animals, nor do they usually visit a corpse until it has lain for a while, so there was little danger of direct conflict between farmers and vultures.

In the 1950s, however, the French authorities decreed that the bodies of dead farm animals should be removed, and buried or burnt, to prevent the spread of disease. Many farmers also believe, perhaps partly as a result of this, that vultures spread diseases, and they have been shot and poisoned as a result. At the same time, the changing pattern of agriculture has meant that fewer animals go onto the hills, and lower percentages of them die each year—currently, about 2 per cent of domestic animals die on the hills each year. Eventually, it was decided that animals which died in the French National Park would be left out for the vultures or other scavengers—though it took an enormous effort on the part of conservationists to achieve this much—and some additional feeding took place. This still left the vultures with a problem, since feeding was stopped each spring as the temperatures rose (to prevent the spread of disease), yet domestic flocks had not yet been put out on to the mountain pastures; this shortage comes just as the vultures are feeding their chicks.

On the Spanish side, things have changed less, since animals are still left where they die, on the grazing grounds; and animals that die in the village are put out onto the local dump for the vultures or feral dogs to find. But there are still gradual changes in agricultural methods going on, and there is still a great deal of ignorance about the role of the vultures in farm hygiene. Great efforts are being made to educate those who would still consider killing vultures, and progress is being made: for the first time in several decades, the numbers of griffon vultures in the Pyrenees is rising again. However, it took a great deal of effort and money on the part of many concerned individuals, sometimes fighting *against* the National Park staff, to protect one large and obvious species. It does not take a great deal of imagination to appreciate how difficult it would be to arrest the decline of many smaller and less obvious species, even if anyone noticed their decline. For conservation to be successful, the whole ecosystem, way of life, and landscape needs to be protected. As yet, this has not happened in the Pyrenees.

66. *Shooting hides on the Col d'Erroymendi, near Larrau. These hides are part of a long line, spaced some 100 m (328 ft) apart, spanning the whole col. The effect on birds migrating over this important low pass can all too easily be imagined.*

Bibliography

For a long time, the literature on the Pyrenees was sparse and scattered, with little of it in English. In the last few years, though, the number of books on the subject has grown enormously, though not all are good, and we list below a selection of those that we have found useful or interesting over the years.

Corbet, G. *The Mammals of Britain and Europe*. Collins, London, 1980.

Davies, P. J. and Huxley, A. *The Wild Orchids of Britain and Europe*. Chatto & Windus, London, 1983.

Grey-Wilson, C. *The Alpine Flowers of Britain and Europe*. Collins, London, 1979.

Grunfeld, F. *Wild Spain*. Ebury Press, London, 1988.

Guides Minvieille du randonneur. Pyrenees Parc National. Fernand Nathan, 1982.

Heinzel, H. *et al. The Birds of Britain and Europe*. Collins, London, 1972.

Higham, Roger *The Pyrenees*. Columbus Books, London, 1988.

Hosea, Bob *et al.* (translators) *Walking the Pyrenees*. GR 10. Robertson McCarta, London, 1989.

Michelin guide: *Spain*. Michelin, Clermont Ferrand, 1985.

———: *Pyrénées Rousillon*. Michelin, 1986 (in French).

———: *Pyrénées Aquitaine*. Michelin, 1986 (in French).

Polunin, O. and Smythies, B. E. *Flowers of South-West Europe: A Field Guide*. Oxford, 1988.

Reynolds, K. *Walks and Climbs in the Pyrenees*. Cicerone Press, Milnthorpe, 1986.

Taylor, A. W. *Wild Flowers of the Pyrenees*. Chatto & Windus, London.

Useful Addresses

WALKING

Association des amis du parc national des Pyrénées—20, rue Samonzet, 64000 Pau.

Accompagnateurs en montagne—guides organizing walks of a day or more in duration:
* Jean-Michel Arizon, 65120 Luz-Saint-Sauveur. *Tel.* 97 83 36
* Serge Pujo Menjouet, 65200 Sainte-Marie-de-Campan.
* Gérard Caubet, 2 impasse de la Fontaine, 65320 Bordères-sur-Echez. *Tel.* 93 93 40.
* Syndicat d'initiative du Biros-Sentein, 09800 Castillon-en-Couserans. *Tel.* (61) 66 73 92.
* Barthélémy Couret, La Tignerie, 31440 Saint-Béat. *Tel.* (61) 79 42 26.
* Jean-Louis Crouzet, avenue de Font-Romeau-Estavar, 66800 Saillagouse.
* Bureau des accompagnateurs, 10 rue du Coustou, 09110 Ax-les-Thermes. *Tel.* (61) 64 21 77.

CENTRES FOR TREKKING AND RIDING

* Auberge cavalière de la vallée d'Aspe, Accous 64490 Bédous. *Tel.* (59) 39 72 30.
* Bilhères-en-Ossau.
* Centre équestre du vallon du Salut, 65200 Bagnères-de-Bigorre. *Tel.* (62) 95 00 05.
* Pony Club de Guchen, 65440 Ancizan. *Tel.* (62) 98 50 02 and 98 50 13.
* Centre équestre de Luchon, 31110 Bagnères-de-Luchon. *Tel.* (61) 79 06 64.

* Ranch Z, Baulou, 09000 Foix.
* Cantegril, Saint-Martin-de-Caralp, 09000 Foix.
* Ranch DD.G., 09310 Les Cabanes.
* Le Soula, 09580 Mérens-les-Vals. *Tel.* (61) 64 24 11.
* Ranch le Fournil, Savignac-les-Ormeaux, 09110 Ax-les-Thermes.
* Centre équestre du Conflent-L'Oustalet, Mas Rigolès, 66500 Prades. *Tel.* (68) 05 14 04.
* Cortal del Manau, Nohèdes, 66500 Prades. *Tel.* (68) 05 23 48.
* Centre équestre de la Laiterie, Vernet-les-Bains, 66500 Prades. *Tel.* 85 52 42.
* Francis Padrosa, Con Sabé, Montbolo, 66100, Amélie-les-Bains. *Tel.* (68) 39 09 09.

MAPS

Edward Stanford Ltd, (Map and guide book stockist), 12–14 Long Acre, London WC2.

McCarta Ltd, (International Map and guide book distributor), 122 Kings Cross Road, London WC1X 9DS.

HOTELS AND ACCOMMODATION

Lists of Hotels, Logis de France, Train and Bus timetables:
French Government Tourist Office, 178 Piccadilly, London W1V 0AI. *Tel.* (071) 491 7622.

Gîtes d'étapes, Refuges and Cabanes—contact: Le Club Alpin Français, 7 rue la Boétie, Paris 75008, France.

Gîtes ruraux, chambres d'hôtes, farm accommodation and farm camping:

* **Pyrénées-Atlantiques:** Association départementales des gîtes ruraux, Chambre d'agriculture, 5 place Marguerite-Laborde, 64000 Pau. *Tel.* (59) 27 98 44.
* **Hautes-Pyrénées:** Association départementales des gîtes ruraux, Maison de l' agriculture, 22 place du Forail, 65000 Tarbes. *Tel.* (62) 93 12 82.
* **Haute-Garonne:** Association départementales des gîtes ruraux, 37 bis, rue Roquelaine, 31000 Toulouse. *Tel.* (61) 62 99 12.
* **Ariège:** Association départementales des gîtes ruraux, Préfecture, 09000 Foix. *Tel.* (61) 65 20 00 (for gîtes ruraux and chambres d'hôtes).

  Service d'utilité agricole et touristique, Chambre d'Agriculture, B.P.53, 09001 Foix. *Tel.* (61) 65 20 00 (for camping on farms).

* **Aude:** Association départementales des gîtes ruraux, 70 rue Aimé-Ramon, 11001 Carcassonne. *Tel.* (68) 25 24 95.
* **Pyrénées-Orientales:** Association départementales des gîtes ruraux, Maison du tourisme du Roussillon, Palais consulaire, 66005 Perpignan. *Tel.* (68) 34 29 94.

YOUTH HOSTELS (AUBERGES DE JEUNESSE)

Youth Hostel Association (YHA), Trevelyan House, St Albans, Herts AL1 2DY, or directly to:

* **Mérens-les-Vals:** 09580 Mérens-les-Vals. *Tel.* (61) 64 24 11.
* **Paletès:** 09200 Saint-Girons. *Tel.* (61) 66 06 79.

Index

(numbers in italics denote illustrations)